WRITERS REPUBLIC L.L.C.
515 Summit Ave. Unit R1
Union City, NJ 07087, USA

Website: *www.writersrepublic.com*
Hotline: *1-877-656-6838*
Email: *info@writersrepublic.com*

Ordering Information:
Quantity sales. Special discounts are available on quantity purchases by corporations, associations, and others. For details, contact the publisher at the address above.

Library of Congress Control Number: 2020948866
ISBN-13:   978-1-64620-750-3   [Paperback Edition]
                  978-1-64620-751-0   [Hardback Edition]
                  978-1-64620-752-7   [Digital Edition]

Rev. date: 10/27/2020

SWAN SONGS OF CYGNUS
THE WEIGHT OF BLACK HOLES

a love story transcending space and time

by

VINCENT HOLLOW

the letter
MAURA KEANEY

the memo
ROBERT V. DOE

the note
JEN SAPORITO

console graphics
planetary vectors
SHAWN MAHONEY

astronaut cover art
TOM NICOSIA

celestial dreamscapes
SOKS GEMMA

FOR ALL THE
Lovers
LOST IN SPACE

AND THE
Stargazers
HERE ON EARTH

SIDE A
Horizons

Interstellar Travels
and Astronomical Relocation
Washington, DC 20546-0001

May 18, 3783

Administrative Offices

TO:

FROM: Dr. Ellen J. Samson
Chief Astrophysicist in charge of
Relocation Program CYGA-79267

SUBJECT: Response to solo manned mission
to the distant quasar, Cygnus A

Mr.

Your proposal for exploration of the ellipsoidal variable star, commonly known to be a black hole, has been reviewed and approved, pending certain conditions are met. Release forms will be mailed to you to gain your acceptance of the conditions listed below. You must follow and approve each step before your mission can proceed.

Please note: acceptance of your proposal does not guarantee the success of your mission. While the expedition has been approved, you are not guaranteed to survive.

. . .

WARNING!
YOU WILL BE TRAVELING TO THE SUPERMASSIVE BLACK HOLE IN THE CENTER OF CYGNUS A. DO NOT APPROACH THE SUPERMASSIVE BLACK HOLE ORBITING THE GALAXY. THAT BLACK HOLE IS UNSTABLE.

FOR BEST CHANCE OF SUCCESS,
DO NOT ENTER THE ORBITAL BLACK HOLE OF CYGNUS A.

Step One: Eyes.

A black hole has extremely high gravitational density. The gravitational pull is so strong, even light cannot escape it. Cygnus A is a radio galaxy that emits a tremendous amount of radio waves in multiple directions. While we do not know the cause, we have observed a steady increase in radio flux density with comparable luminosity to the brightest known supernova. Due to the brightness emitted from Cygnus A and the absolute absence of light within its central supermassive black hole, you will need specialized light-sensitive ocular nerves.

We must replace your organic eyes with inorganic implants. A special blend of polymer strings and metal wire will connect the new eyes to your brain, through the optical nerve, using the electrical synapses. The polymer will grow and weave into the dural folds of the brain, allowing your eyes to work properly without performing brain surgery.

The ocular implants will include an artificial intelligence system, henceforth called AI, to assist in the logistics of space travel and help stave off insanity caused by long periods of isolation. The AI will communicate with you and interface seamlessly with the ship. It will be integrated with your brain to allow it to communicate with you should there be a malfunction with the ship. The AI will also moderate your daily medication (See Step Three). Traveling a distance of 600 million lightyears without human interaction or outside stimuli can cause mental instability. The AI will counteract this by acting as your companion, and performing the duties of a qualified scientist on board.

To shorten the time it takes to get to Cygnus A and the black hole at its center, you will travel at lightspeed within the solar system until you reach the orbit of Pluto within the Kuiper Belt, at which point you will activate your vessel's warp drive. The AI will navigate and monitor the fuel, should you need to pass an emission nebula to absorb the high-energy photons to keep the vessel going at such speeds.

Step Two: Bones.

Cygnus A is a quasar, a galactic X-ray and radio source. You will be exposed to larger doses of radiation the closer you get to the black hole. You will need to prepare your body to survive your mission. All black holes emit radiation, but Cygnus A also emits jets of energy that heat intergalactic gas in galaxy clusters and prevent it from cooling and forming large numbers of stars.

To counteract the radiation and the negative affect it will have on your body, your bone marrow will be injected with chelators that will bind to actinides to form large, stable complexes that are easier for the body to expel. Bone marrow extraction can be extremely painful and you will be in an airtight clean room for the duration of the surgery and subsequent healing process.

The long duration of your mission will cause bone decay, mostly in your joints. You will have your joints replaced with a molybdenum steel alloy. The alloy joints are strong and last long after organic joints would deteriorate. The molybdenum steel alloy will not absorb the radiation as much as other alloys, nor will it melt in your body like a plastic counterpart. While it typically would be prudent to replace all of your bones with this compound, you need organic material for your bone marrow to be infused with the chelator.

Step Three: Daily Medication.

You will need to stop the oxidation of your organs and overuse of your muscles. To achieve this, you will take a daily injection of tetrodotoxin in a very small dose, a saline solution containing vitamins and minerals that preserve tissue and organic matter, and small doses of formaldehyde and other preservatives. The tetrodotoxin will stop your muscles from working. The AI and ocular implant will regulate your nervous system so the tetrodotoxin can work on preserving your muscles from overuse and decay. The saline will dilute the poison, keep your body hydrated, and help you absorb the vital proteins and minerals you need to keep you healthy. The formaldehyde and other preservatives, again, in very small doses, will also prevent decay.

Because of the instabilities of the medication's components, it requires a very specific dose. It is a very precise medication that can kill you if you take too much or too little. The AI will make sure the dosages are precise. Before you leave on your journey, you must practice with the AI to dose out the medication accurately. The dose will be tested by a team of scientists until you and the AI perfect it. Being in sync with the AI will ensure a safe expedition.

Please note, once again, acceptance of your proposal does not guarantee the success of your expedition. While the expedition has been approved, you are not guaranteed to survive. You will soon observe things no human eyes have seen up close. Your journey will take you to a distant galaxy, passing all known planets of our solar system, luminous and vivid nebulae, and every other celestial body that most scientists only dream of seeing up close.

If our conditions are amenable to you, the expedition will go on as planned. Come to the facility noted in the release forms by 8:00 am Monday morning so we can begin your enhancements without delay. If you do not wish to proceed with the aforementioned procedures, then thank you for interest in traveling to Cygnus A, however we must rescind our approval.

Have a great day and we look forward to training you for this exciting exploration.

Ellen J. Samson
Head Astrophysicist of Relocation Program

PATRICK CHRISTOPHERSON
Director

Civilian Relations
& Recruitment Office

June 22, 3783

When you stopped returning my calls, I felt it was my
place as your friend to grant you the space and time
you needed. It is one of the advantages of holding the
position I do that I'm more qualified than most to
judge what a person in your position might need. Space
and time, I thought… but not like this. The irony, you
see, has struck me. It would be funny was it not so
sad.

I was alerted when your application arrived, of
course. It came across my desk weeks ago. And the
chill it sent down my spine, the temporary rigor
mortis (perhaps these superfluous ironies are not lost
on you) could not deter me from doing the cold task
which was my charge, to determine whether you, a
civilian, with no formal training in space travel or
external data collection, were mentally fit to undergo
the radical mission for which you had volunteered.

Having never been willing to entertain your threats to do so, having mourned, in my own way, our loss (for it was our loss ██████████ - you must know that) and, of course, having not spoken to you in several months, well - despite my professional and personal reservations, I had no proper recourse, no excuse, really, to deny your application. You are a bit broken, my friend, but you are not crazy. All told, you rank high in attentiveness and reliability, though not as high as you once did, and you are, in point of fact, a better candidate for the mission than most.

And so, with stiff limbs and a dry tongue, I stood before the board and announced that this civilian, relatively unknown by the INSTAR elite, this writer, newly bereaved, was mentally fit to join our program. I did so with all due formality, and never said what was on my mind, that this man was sad and lonely, that he was desperate and withdrawn - I never said that he was my friend.

But I'll say it now, ██████████ I'll tell you now, in case we never speak again, that when I performed what I felt was my duty, I never believed you'd be accepted with your lack of formal training. And I never believed, if you were, that, having been informed of the necessary biological upgrades and the dangers, nevermind the infinitesimal chance of success, that you would actually subject yourself to this process.

By now, your joints, bone marrow, and eyes have been removed. As empty as you must have felt these past months, you are emptier now more than you've ever been. That is why I sit here, at the same desk where I first laid eyes on your application, typing this grave letter in darkness. Because I cannot speak to you.

I took time today to walk down the long white
corridors to the medical wing. You've heard me speak
of them many times. I spent my early years in training
there. I have even lectured there. The medical wing's
corridors have always been a place of reverence for
me, a place to reminisce and reflect on the immense
advances we've made. But when I walked those corridors
today, it was in earnest and in haste. Finding Room
143, I entered, and found your cryotube, and I looked
down at you, deflated and half-there, effectively
dead, with the toxins dripping, almost frozen, from
your empty eyes. I touched the glass.

It felt almost the same. You looked like her. And the
pain I felt then - the pain I feel now - well, perhaps
I know why.

It is too late now to stop you. But I never got to say
good-bye. So good-bye, my friend.

Forgive me.

                              - Pat

My very essence is fading away, like sand crystals through an hourglass. I wish it didn't have to be like this. Its never easy to say goodbye, to watch someone go while here you stay. But, my heart is open, like the night sky opens to expose the stars to us. keep your heart open, as well. remember those nights. When the light of the moon shines down and touches your skin, feel my love. when the evening wind dances by your ear, hear my words. we are but stardust, my love. glorious, wonderous, stardust. until our stars cross again, i'll be waiting.

all my love

Lucy

CYGNUS A TRAJECTORY
PHASE ONE: THE TERRESTRIAL PLANETS

TREBLE

PRE-
FLIGHT

LAUNCH

VENUS

everything starts
as dreams
and stars

EARTH

MARS

ENTER
ASTEROID

BASS

POWER

TRAJ

TUNER

VOLUME

ORIGINS

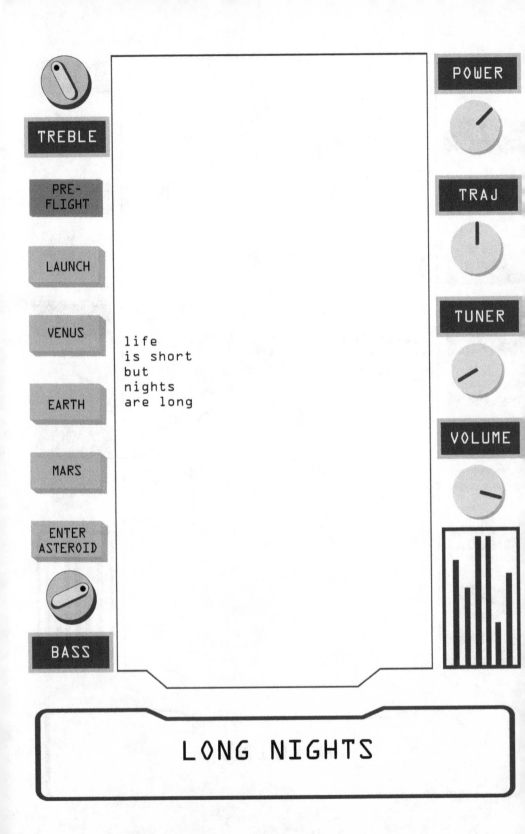

life
is short
but
nights
are long

TREBLE

PRE-
FLIGHT

LAUNCH

VENUS

EARTH

MARS

ENTER
ASTEROID

BASS

first there was nothing
and then BANG! you came along
you were ev'rything

POWER

TRAJ

TUNER

VOLUME

BIG BANG

TREBLE

PRE-
FLIGHT

LAUNCH

VENUS

EARTH

MARS

ENTER
ASTEROID

BASS

everything I do revolves around

YOU

POWER

TRAJ

TUNER

VOLUME

REVOLVE

TREBLE

PRE-
FLIGHT

LAUNCH

VENUS

EARTH

MARS

ENTER
ASTEROID

BASS

we have water
to swim in
to keep us alive

we have fire
to warm our bodies
and ward off the night

we have air
to laugh and scream
and sing

we have the earth
as a home
a place to begin

but what we need
more than anything
is love

POWER

TRAJ

TUNER

VOLUME

THE FIFTH ELEMENT

TREBLE

PRE-FLIGHT

LAUNCH

VENUS

EARTH

MARS

ENTER ASTEROID

BASS

far away from here
a new home among the spheres
all my bones replaced
no sound when they break

the sky graduates
through every shade of blue
until it finally turns black
my electric eyes dilate
adjusting to the dimming hues
as I finalize the soundtrack

no way to tell
if I'm awake or dreaming
the helmet, my shell
am I singing or screaming?

the phases of the moon
the dunes of Mars
you and I always in tune
with the rotation of stars

meteors violently pass
ricocheting off the windows
that cradle my final words to you
a hovercraft in a bottle of glass
your love safely enclosed
your ghost forever pursued

the cracks slowly slither
tatters in the sails
Hydra shakes winter
from its severed scales

I do not know
the meaning of the zodiac
but what I do know is
I will be back

POWER

TRAJ

TUNER

VOLUME

ESCAPE VELOCITY

TREBLE

PRE-
FLIGHT

LAUNCH

VENUS

EARTH

MARS

ENTER
ASTEROID

BASS

POWER

TRAJ

TUNER

VOLUME

firing like a spectral bullet
through the heart of space
but it is never mentioned
in scientific studies
the speed of the Dark

for the light comes
and the light goes
but the Dark
the Dark comes
and the Dark
it tends
to linger

   AND FOR THAT, YOU WILL NEED
   AN ENTIRELY DIFFERENT VESSEL

the Dark consumes
a tremendous wave
of velvet murder
a smothering blanket held
by the frigid hands
of this artificial skeleton
a carnivorous force
with an appetite
for the faintest of glows
you keep safely inside

it is a phantom ventriloquist
possessive, manipulative
it's the voice on the radio
it's the air in the oxygen tank
it's the fuel in the shuttle

the Dark comes
the Dark lingers
the Dark comes
the Dark lingers

THE SPEED OF LIGHT

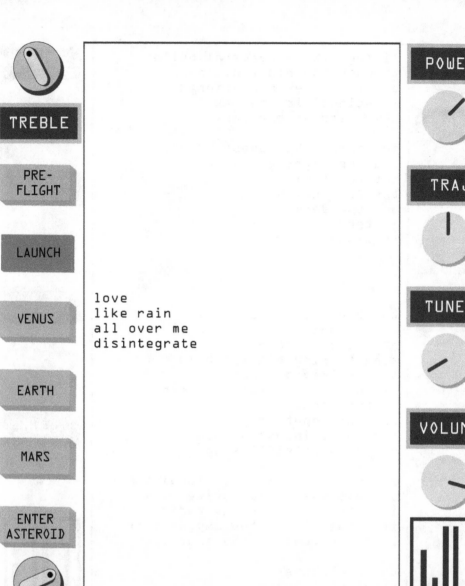

TREBLE

PRE-
FLIGHT

LAUNCH

VENUS

EARTH

MARS

ENTER
ASTEROID

BASS

love
like rain
all over me
disintegrate

POWER

TRAJ

TUNER

VOLUME

AQUARIDS

TREBLE

PRE-
FLIGHT

LAUNCH

VENUS

EARTH

MARS

ENTER
ASTEROID

BASS

POWER

TRAJ

TUNER

VOLUME

if it takes more than a lifetime
searching through this verse
our surrogate children
will follow in my footsteps
generation after generation
until you are found

GENERATION SHIP

VENUS

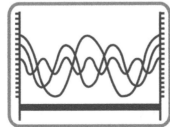

TREBLE

PRE-
FLIGHT

LAUNCH

VENUS

EARTH

MARS

ENTER
ASTEROID

BASS

POWER

TRAJ

TUNER

VOLUME

"Is it true that Venus was once
very similar to Earth?"

IT WAS. IT HAD CONTINENTS,
OCEANS, AND EVEN A BREATHABLE
ATMOSPHERE. BUT A RUNAWAY
GREENHOUSE EFFECT TURNED IT INTO
THE HOTTEST PLANET IN OUR SYSTEM,
DESPITE BEING SECOND FROM THE SUN

"Is that why some
call it Planet Hell?"

I WOULD NOT KNOW
ANYTHING ABOUT THAT

VENUS INTERFACE

TREBLE

PRE-
FLIGHT

LAUNCH

VENUS

EARTH

MARS

ENTER
ASTEROID

BASS

POWER

TRAJ

TUNER

VOLUME

sunrise to sunset
pyroclastic flow
my morningstar
years quick, days slow

you're the burn I need
my first tattoo
glacial heart melts
climate won't change you

as we kiss
swan songs fly from our lungs
smoke and lyrics on our lips
twirling with our tongues

flesh evaporates
forecast of acid rain
volcanic eruptions
lava tube veins

everything burns
cigarettes and daydreams
the sweet taste of
chocolate-flavored gasoline

VENUS

TREBLE

PRE-
FLIGHT

LAUNCH

VENUS

EARTH

MARS

ENTER
ASTEROID

BASS

POWER

TRAJ

TUNER

VOLUME

the surface of Venus
is hot enough
to melt lead
your touch
is hot enough
to melt my bones

THE MELTING POINT OF LEAD

TREBLE

PRE-
FLIGHT

LAUNCH

VENUS

EARTH

MARS

ENTER
ASTEROID

BASS

POWER

TRAJ

TUNER

VOLUME

the water is hot
but you were always hotter
and somehow
I was immune
to your sultry skin

your heat
turns the rain to steam
robbing my mouth of moisture
as I stand, jaw on the tiles
in the presence of such carnality

my tongue
collects the water
along every contour and curve
like a thirsty lizard
inebriated by your taste

ACID RAIN

POWER

TREBLE

TRAJ

PRE-
FLIGHT

LAUNCH

TUNER

VENUS

EARTH

VOLUME

MARS

ENTER
ASTEROID

BASS

punctured heart
arrows tickle ribcage
sensation of blossoms
and butterfly kisses

sunbathing on Venus
melting wax sculpture
coiled in acid rain
love's contagious fumes

flames of lightning
charcoal heart
chest bursts
unexpected host

it all happened so fast
the moment I laid
my young blue eyes
on you

CHEST BURST

E A R T H

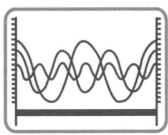

TREBLE

PRE-
FLIGHT

LAUNCH

VENUS

EARTH

MARS

ENTER
ASTEROID

BASS

POWER

TRAJ

TUNER

VOLUME

"It's a bittersweet feeling
knowing this is the last time
I'll see Earth again."

ARE YOU HAVING SECOND THOUGHTS?

"About the mission?"

ABOUT ANY OF THIS, I SUPPOSE

"I've had a million thoughts
since then. Of everything before,
of everything to come."

WHAT HAVE YOU CONCLUDED?

"She deserves this."

DESERVES WHAT?

"To be found."

EARTH INTERFACE

TREBLE

POWER

TRAJ

PRE-
FLIGHT

LAUNCH

TUNER

VENUS

VOLUME

EARTH

MARS

ENTER
ASTEROID

BASS

was it twenty degrees
toward Andromeda or Cassiopeia?
never got to see
those autumn leaves

I remember our house
I remember our street
should have taken another route

same sky, same floor
but the people
no more

images from the video archives
seem a little synthetic
are these the correct files?

samples analyzed
chain reaction
error in the hard drive?

GLITCH IN THE SYSTEM PERHAPS

it says this place is home
but it can't be
if I still feel so alone

ALIEN

photographer of the dead
nocturnal necromancer
exorcist of xrays
constellation collector

I stare long into the night
and see only the past
within your redshift-eyes
fading too fast

just out of reach
safe on my memory disc
secrets of the lanterns
you are worth the risk

keep burning, love
it's never too late
to set things right
please radiate

HUBBLE

TREBLE

PRE-
FLIGHT

LAUNCH

VENUS

EARTH

MARS

ENTER
ASTEROID

BASS

```
I could tell you
infinitely
melodically
how much I love you

how enamored I am
to look upon you
knowing you are mine
and no one else's

but you leave me awestruck
lyrical rhymes allude me
in a voice out of tune
all you hear is the metronome

          BEEP
               BEEP
                    BEEP

my heart's way of saying

            "I love you."
```

SPUTNIK

TREBLE

PRE-
FLIGHT

LAUNCH

VENUS

EARTH

MARS

ENTER
ASTEROID

BASS

your radiance jettisons
across the cosmos
and collides with my heart
of crystals and frost
ultraviolet becomes ultraviolent

but the ribbons and rainbows
ripple and weave
through the night
like a gentle river flowing
with all the colors of your eyes

I'm not sure
if it's the death of seasons
or your radioactive exuberance
that steals the breath
from my lungs

but there's a spark
left by a solar flare
cauterizing all the wounds
left by the moon

wrap me in your curtains
like gauze to my scars
keep me safe
keep me warm

POWER

TRAJ

TUNER

VOLUME

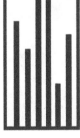

AURORA BOREALIS

TREBLE

PRE-
FLIGHT

LAUNCH

VENUS

EARTH

MARS

ENTER
ASTEROID

BASS

POWER

TRAJ

TUNER

VOLUME

```
in the sky
staring at stars
are you out there
waiting for me?
blink so I can see you
so I can find you
```

KEPLER

M O O N

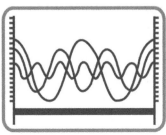
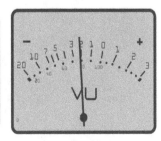

TREBLE

POWER

PRE-
FLIGHT

TRAJ

THE MOON SHOULD BE
COMING UP ON THE LEFT

"You think we can see the
Man on the Moon from here?"

LAUNCH

THERE HAS BEEN A FUNCTIONING
MOON BASE FOR SEVERAL DECADES.
THERE IS MORE THAN JUST ONE
MAN ON THE MOON

TUNER

VENUS

"This is supposed to be
some kind of feature. Like a
crater or something."

EARTH

I DO NOT HAVE ANYTHING
IN MY DATABASE ABOUT
ANY SUCH FEATURE

VOLUME

MARS

"Maybe it was destroyed during
the base's construction."

PERHAPS

ENTER
ASTEROID

BASS

MOON INTERFACE

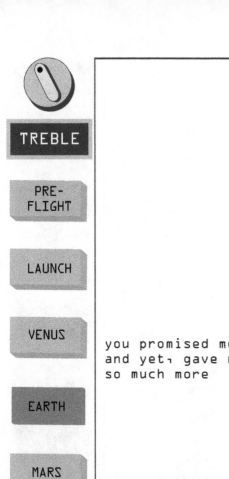

TREBLE

PRE-
FLIGHT

LAUNCH

VENUS

EARTH

MARS

ENTER
ASTEROID

BASS

POWER

TRAJ

TUNER

VOLUME

you promised me the moon
and yet, gave me
so much more

THE MOON

TREBLE

POWER

PRE-
FLIGHT

TRAJ

LAUNCH

VENUS

TUNER

EARTH

MARS

VOLUME

ENTER
ASTEROID

BASS

```
missing pieces
polaroid past
crooked timeline
shutter and flash

how long has it been
since we walked along the shore
as the moon and the tides
erase our footprints once more?

sugar lips dissolved
only salt on wounded words
filling lungs unsealed
with the sound of dying birds
```

TIDES

TREBLE

PRE-
FLIGHT

LAUNCH

VENUS

EARTH

MARS

ENTER
ASTEROID

BASS

timelines and lifelines
changing tides
sand in the seas
crash and recede

ancient runes
simulated wounds
altered shape
foreign landscape

find serenity
Sea of Tranquility
on the dark side
voices amplified

crescent smile
your ghost's exile
wax to wane
love over pain

tides of change
molecules rearranged
time after time
always be mine

POWER

TRAJ

TUNER

VOLUME

PHASES

TREBLE

POWER

bodies in space
the black swan's ballet
sunlight erased
I won't look away

   "Blackout the sun with me."

my heart will become molten
no longer frozen
and the crust will combust
to thunderous eruptions
clouds of CO_2
me and you

summer rain heals
like alcohol to a razor's kiss
the relief I feel
when I reminisce

PRE-
FLIGHT

TRAJ

LAUNCH

TUNER

VENUS

EARTH

VOLUME

MARS

ENTER
ASTEROID

BASS

ECLIPSES

MARS

 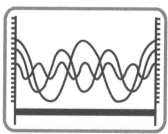 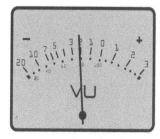

TREBLE

POWER

PRE-
FLIGHT

TRAJ

LAUNCH

"It's so strange to think about.
This place was once a desert
hundreds of years ago."

THE COLONIZATION OF MARS
WAS AN IMPORTANT STEP
FOR YOUR ANCESTORS.
TERRAFORMING THE PLANET,
HOWEVER, IS ANOTHER
FEAT ENTIRELY

VENUS

TUNER

EARTH

"Do you think it's possible
to bring a planet back
from the dead?"

WITH TIME, PATIENCE, AND
THE PROPER TECHNOLOGY,
I CANNOT SEE WHY NOT

MARS

VOLUME

"What about a person?"

UNABLE TO CLARIFY

ENTER
ASTEROID

BASS

MARS INTERFACE

TREBLE

PRE-
FLIGHT

LAUNCH

VENUS

EARTH

MARS

ENTER
ASTEROID

BASS

blood on skin
leaving a stain
no water
can wash away

WELL IT COULD,
BUT ALL THE WATER
TURNED TO SAND LONG AGO

I look back at you
and see how I once was
I fear someday you'll be dead
someday you'll be red

I am a desert
no one stays for too long
couldn't take care of myself
so how could I sustain you?

extracting the lifeforce
pour over the frozen terrain
it is your life
that gives me life

attempts at contact
bring only static to my ears
let the desert winds
erase all evidence of you

because nothing
can take me back
to the way I was
back then

. . .

I remember the day
you turned red
I remember the day you were

POWER

TRAJ

TUNER

VOLUME

MARS

TREBLE

PRE-
FLIGHT

LAUNCH

VENUS

EARTH

MARS

ENTER
ASTEROID

BASS

I want to take this opportunity
to explore your deserts
dust storms of past heartbreaks
riverbeds of rust
in empty canyons

you will be my mission
my priority one
I will prove to you
the existence of love
by giving you all of mine

POWER

TRAJ

TUNER

VOLUME

OPPORTUNITY

TREBLE

PRE-
FLIGHT

LAUNCH

VENUS

EARTH

MARS

ENTER
ASTEROID

BASS

POWER

TRAJ

TUNER

VOLUME

I want the canyons to echo
a different voice
because mine is so lost
in the stone labyrinths
and dried up riverbeds
how can it know
if the voice it hears
isn't yours?

VALLES MARINERIS

TREBLE

PRE-
FLIGHT

LAUNCH

VENUS

EARTH

MARS

ENTER
ASTEROID

BASS

I watched you disintegrate
but I couldn't let you go
the pieces of you abandoned me
leaving me a cemetery sky
with only dead stars to wish upon

I looked up
into the great oblivion
I wished for you to stay
I wished you were everywhere

gazing in awe
as your remnants gathered
in a celestial maypole dance
forming a spectacular ring
of our infinite unity
in this life and the next

POWER

TRAJ

TUNER

VOLUME

PHOBOS

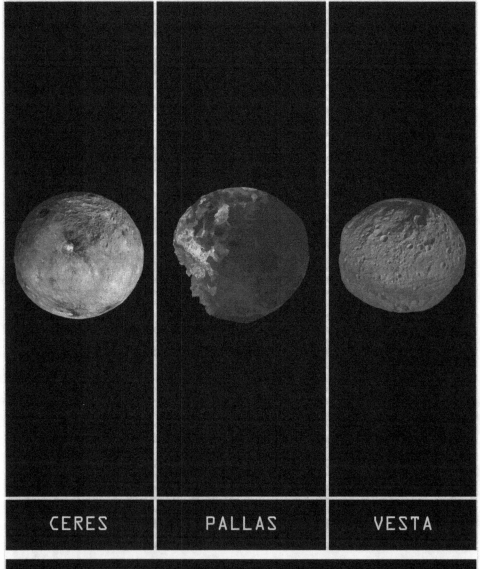

CERES   PALLAS   VESTA

A S T E R O I D   B E L T

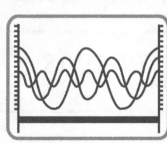

TREBLE

PRE-
FLIGHT

LAUNCH

VENUS

EARTH

MARS

ENTER
ASTEROID

BASS

here at the wall
guards stand at their posts
watching the giants sleepwalk
in steady orbits

Trojans and Centaurs
pace the perimeter
they keep me safe
they keep me sane

there are spaces
in-between mortar and stone
wide enough to squeeze through,
vessel intact,
to the infinite

POWER

TRAJ

TUNER

VOLUME

ASTEROID BELT

CYGNUS A TRAJECTORY
PHASE TWO: THE GAS + ICE GIANTS

TREBLE

EXIT
ASTEROID

JUPITER

SATURN

URANUS

NEPTUNE

ENTER
KUIPER

BASS

POWER

TRAJ

TUNER

VOLUME

I'll take the stars down for you
all the planets
all the moons

they sing to you
echoing the elegy
of our swans' tormented tune

composing our universe for you
inside the lid
of your cryotube

CRYOTUBE A

JUPITER

 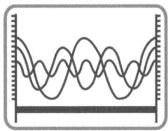 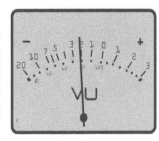

TREBLE

EXIT
ASTEROID

JUPITER

SATURN

URANUS

NEPTUNE

ENTER
KUIPER

BASS

"Isn't there supposed to be
a red spot around here
somewhere?"

MY DATA SHOWS THAT STORM
DISAPPEARED IN THE YEAR 2030

"Guess that's something
we have in common."

WHAT IS THAT?

"We've both lost something.
Something that was once
a part of us."

I CAN BRING UP SOME IMAGES
IF YOU WOULD LIKE TO SEE

"Where did you find
images of her?"

HER?

POWER

TRAJ

TUNER

VOLUME

JUPITER INTERFACE

TREBLE

EXIT
ASTEROID

JUPITER

SATURN

URANUS

NEPTUNE

ENTER
KUIPER

BASS

your hair's on fire
drawn by nuclear fusion
cheeks bloom gold
fingers comb your coronal loops
blister and char my palms

there would be more to you
than just hydrogen and helium
inside, it's waiting
I couldn't look away
even if I wanted to

the star you were meant to be
had all unraveled
woven flames undone
now there is only the beast

POWER

TRAJ

TUNER

VOLUME

JUPITER

TREBLE

EXIT
ASTEROID

JUPITER

SATURN

URANUS

NEPTUNE

ENTER
KUIPER

BASS

threw my heart
in a blender
set the dial to
"Hurricane"

toss in
the flesh
and all
the bones

AT LEAST WHAT IS LEFT OF THEM

watching, unfazed
at this torrent of torment
feeding eternally
on everything I was

POWER

TRAJ

TUNER

VOLUME

THE GREAT RED SPOT

TREBLE

EXIT
ASTEROID

JUPITER

SATURN

URANUS

NEPTUNE

ENTER
KUIPER

BASS

```
caught in your embrace
holding on tightly
you and I
falling together

breaking into pieces
of glass and icicle tears
you and I
falling together

incinerating
upon the first impact
we continued our descent
falling forever
```

POWER

TRAJ

TUNER

VOLUME

SHOEMAKER-LEVY 9

TREBLE

EXIT
ASTEROID

JUPITER

SATURN

URANUS

NEPTUNE

ENTER
KUIPER

BASS

POWER

TRAJ

TUNER

VOLUME

probing eyes
penetrate through
savage, unforgiving clouds
of unfathomable magnitude
glistening streaks of gold
passing over you
to catch a glimpse
of your hazel eyes
it's so hard
to see you like this

JUNO

TREBLE

EXIT
ASTEROID

JUPITER

SATURN

URANUS

NEPTUNE

ENTER
KUIPER

BASS

```
temperature rising
I can't stop sweating
heart burning wildly
hypnotized by you
frozen in the video monitor
wondering if you see me too
you're the match
strike me hard
make the bruises last
I erupt, you explode
ice caps melt
landscapes erode
```

POWER

TRAJ

TUNER

VOLUME

IO

TREBLE

EXIT
ASTEROID

JUPITER

SATURN

URANUS

NEPTUNE

ENTER
KUIPER

BASS

millions of miles between us
telescopic images of you,
my arctic satellite,
reveal the lingering scars
from your malady's fingernails

magnetic field draws you in
warming your carbonite heart
as you had first done to mine
when we were only particles
alone and blind in the deep

you have such oceans within you
I swan dive every night
into the silent abyss
searching diligently
for any possible signs of life

for where there is water
there is always life

POWER

TRAJ

TUNER

VOLUME

EUROPA

SATURN

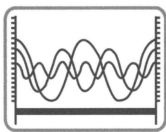

TREBLE

EXIT
ASTEROID

JUPITER

SATURN

URANUS

NEPTUNE

ENTER
KUIPER

BASS

POWER

TRAJ

TUNER

VOLUME

"They were right."

ABOUT WHAT?

"It being so beautiful."

MANY SAY IT IS THE
MOST BEAUTIFUL CELESTIAL
OBJECT IN OUR SYSTEM

"That's too bad."

WHY IS THAT?

"They never saw her."

SATURN INTERFACE

TREBLE

EXIT
ASTEROID

JUPITER

SATURN

URANUS

NEPTUNE

ENTER
KUIPER

BASS

floating on the surface
rings on her fingers
she remembers the names
of all her moons

backstroking in a sea of stars
enraptured by the galaxies
and globular clusters
dancing above her head

spreading her arms to fly
but unable to escape
from the power of gravity
pulling her back into darkness

warming our drifting bodies
in the light of Deneb
we'll bask in eternal summer
aboard our private vessel

and instead of floating
we would soar, my love
our feathers intertwined
in our swan ballet

POWER

TRAJ

TUNER

VOLUME

SATURN

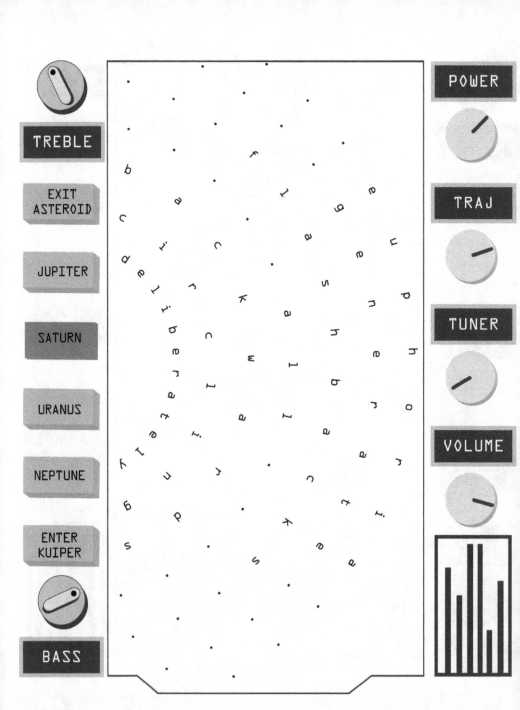

TREBLE

POWER

dance with me, love
in every season
be the summer
in our winter waltz
sprinkle snowflakes like sugar

taste their sweetness
as I kiss you
softly in the drifts
so you can't tell the difference
between the snow and my lips

EXIT
ASTEROID

TRAJ

dance with me, love
from the kitchen
sliding in our socks
like inebriated ice skaters
to the bedroom

JUPITER

SATURN

stumbling around dirty clothes
attempting to keep rhythm
before we collapse
on our queen-size mattress

TUNER

URANUS

dance with me, love
behind eyelid curtains
on a supernova stage
my ballerina in my brain

VOLUME

NEPTUNE

whisper in my ear
the language of memories
spinning slowly to a stop
as the curtain descends
and I don't want to wake up

ENTER
KUIPER

BASS

DIONE + ENCELADUS

TREBLE

EXIT
ASTEROID

JUPITER

SATURN

URANUS

NEPTUNE

ENTER
KUIPER

BASS

```
our first father
takes all
and leaves none
we are all his children
we are all his victims

we get so dizzy
watching his hands
spinning eternally
full of greetings
and goodbyes

titan of titans
consumes us all
merciless, unsympathetic
we are all his children
we are all his victims
```

POWER

TRAJ

TUNER

VOLUME

CRONUS

TREBLE

EXIT
ASTEROID

JUPITER

SATURN

URANUS

NEPTUNE

ENTER
KUIPER

BASS

beneath thick nitrogen clouds
lurking in hydrocarbon canyons
navigating ethane rivers
I'm still here with you, love

even if you appear
as a Van Gogh portrait
through my fog-draped eyes
I'll always remember
the way you were

and it's one of the only things
I have left, my love
that makes me carry on
with a smile

POWER

TRAJ

TUNER

VOLUME

TITAN

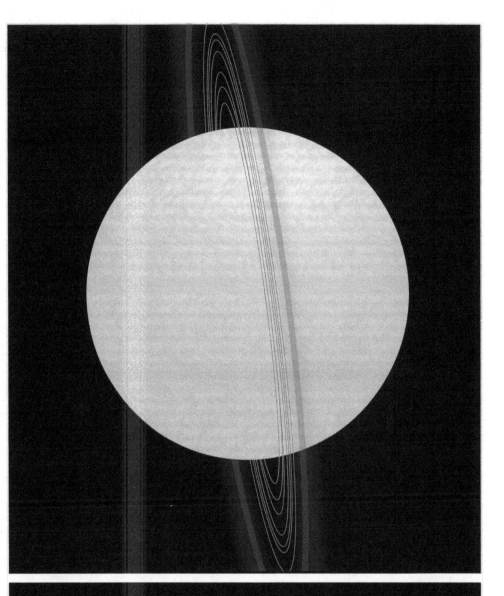

URANUS

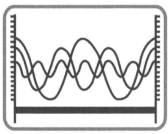

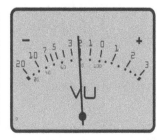

TREBLE

POWER

TRAJ

TUNER

VOLUME

EXIT
ASTEROID

JUPITER

SATURN

URANUS

NEPTUNE

ENTER
KUIPER

BASS

"Strange how it rotates
on its side like that."

RESEARCH SHOWS ANOTHER PLANETARY
OBJECT COLLIDED WITH URANUS
DURING ITS EARLY FORMATION

"Kind of how it was
when we first met."

HOW SO?

"It didn't take long after that
for her to knock me off my feet.
Feeling disoriented, but enjoying
what I saw from this new
perspective. You know what I
mean?"

I DO NOT BELIEVE I HAVE HAD
THAT PROGRAMMED IN MY SYSTEM

"I'll tell you
about it sometime."

URANUS INTERFACE

TREBLE

EXIT
ASTEROID

JUPITER

SATURN

URANUS

NEPTUNE

ENTER
KUIPER

BASS

POWER

TRAJ

TUNER

VOLUME

violent collision
views askew
blurred vision
reversed latitude

you are the sky
your head in the clouds
moonlight eyes
whisper winds resound

butterflies and drones
flutter in my stomach
voice on the telephone
can't escape from it

DO NOT FORGET TO TAKE YOUR PILL

heart of comet ice
thaws in torch song flares
the color of the northern lights
they couldn't help but stare

. . .

the aroma of erosion
a murder crowing
no antidote to the poison
the winds keep blowing

URANUS

TREBLE

EXIT
ASTEROID

JUPITER

SATURN

URANUS

NEPTUNE

ENTER
KUIPER

BASS

POWER

TRAJ

TUNER

VOLUME

in my cryochamber
toss and turn
restless and anxious
backwards and upside down
hard to tell where I'm headed
is the trajectory correct?

the giant approaches
I greet him
and request permission
for safe passage
through his kingdom
of ice and wind

DISORIENTED

TREBLE

POWER

an odd array of emotions
the flashbacks
become a flash flood
unable to catch my breath
before the next wave hits

artificial gravity keeps my head
from spinning off my shoulders
but I find myself head over heels
for the second time

a puff of smoke, a flash of light
a magician's assistant
in a spellbound box
emerges a swan-shaped cloud

passing over you
I take it all in
the good and the bad
and regretting neither

EXIT
ASTEROID

JUPITER

SATURN

URANUS

NEPTUNE

ENTER
KUIPER

TRAJ

TUNER

VOLUME

BASS

FLASHES

TREBLE

EXIT
ASTEROID

JUPITER

SATURN

URANUS

NEPTUNE

ENTER
KUIPER

BASS

my love
sonnets will be written
in your honor, someday
songs sung by fairies
fluttering fireflies
in a midsummer night's dream

your love
soft and poetic
a cooing lullaby
in a frost-laced forest
I hear it through the trees
I taste it on the snow

our love
will endure
long after the stars
whimper away
for you and I are vessels
made of stardust

POWER

TRAJ

TUNER

VOLUME

JULIET

NEPTUNE

 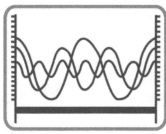 

TREBLE

EXIT
ASTEROID

JUPITER

SATURN

URANUS

NEPTUNE

ENTER
KUIPER

BASS

ACCORDING TO MY CALCULATIONS,
WE SHOULD REACH PLUTO IN ABOUT
FIVE HOURS IF OUR CURRENT SPEED
REMAINS CONSTANT

"Too bad this is the only time
I'll ever get to see our solar
system. I would have liked
to come back."

ALL IMAGES AND VIDEO FOOTAGE OF
THE PLANETARY FLYBYS HAVE BEEN
AUTOMATICALLY SAVED TO THE
VESSEL'S COMPUTER. YOU HAVE
COMPLETE ACCESS TO VIEW THEM AT
ANY POINT DURING THE MISSION

"A photograph isn't the same
as seeing the real thing
with your own eyes."

BUT YOU DO NOT
HAVE YOUR OWN EYES

"You know what I mean."

POWER

TRAJ

TUNER

VOLUME

NEPTUNE INTERFACE

TREBLE

POWER

frail and cold, arms folded
in the shape of an X
in the Black Swan
my sleeping beauty rests

a chasm of infinity
and supersonic winds
without you, love
how again do I begin?

how will I tell your mother
your stagnant heart
is among the astral catacombs?
how did you get so far?

the faint essence of you
sleeps under a Tritonian shell
I was never well-trained
in calculations or farewells

EXIT
ASTEROID

TRAJ

JUPITER

TUNER

SATURN

VOLUME

URANUS

NEPTUNE

ENTER
KUIPER

BASS

NEPTUNE

POWER

TREBLE

EXIT
ASTEROID

TRAJ

JUPITER

SATURN

TUNER

URANUS

NEPTUNE

VOLUME

ENTER
KUIPER

BASS

maiden of the sea
a long-forgotten city
below the waves
sleeping within coral caves

everyone told me
I was crazy
you couldn't be saved
it was already too late

I had to believe
you were waiting for me
a wandering ghost in the mist
lips twinkle from our last kiss

ATLANTIS

TREBLE

EXIT
ASTEROID

JUPITER

SATURN

URANUS

NEPTUNE

ENTER
KUIPER

BASS

diamond cry
ocean blue
eyes like skies
the wells of youth
ocean deep
diamond rain
a promise to keep
we'll meet again

POWER

TRAJ

TUNER

VOLUME

TRITON

TREBLE

EXIT
ASTEROID

JUPITER

SATURN

URANUS

NEPTUNE

ENTER
KUIPER

BASS

the universe
is dark and deep
and I have lightyears to go
before we meet

SEARCHING
"ROBERT FROST POEMS"...

a mermaid, iridescent
in a sea-salt snow globe
her voice bubbles
and her songs float

bioluminescent stars

"When did it get so cold?"

drawing constellations
while wearing a blindfold

if the sky
continues changing
I shall remain lost
while you keep waiting

POWER

TRAJ

TUNER

VOLUME

THE DEEP

TREBLE

EXIT ASTEROID

JUPITER

SATURN

URANUS

NEPTUNE

ENTER KUIPER

BASS

knees buckle
spine shakes
I'll pick you up
the earth quakes

lungs exhale
heartbeat slows
in me, our love
forever glows

brain caves under
insurmountable weight
be there for me
always wait

typhoon winds carry me
further away from you
be my Polaris, love
bring home your boy of blue

POWER

TRAJ

TUNER

VOLUME

THE GREAT DARK SPOT

TREBLE

EXIT ASTEROID

JUPITER

SATURN

URANUS

NEPTUNE

ENTER KUIPER

BASS

POWER

TRAJ

TUNER

VOLUME

```
       THIS IS A ONE-WAY TRIP
       THERE IS NO COMING BACK

     "I'm cold and I'm scared."

   YOU THINK YOU ARE SCARED NOW?
         JUST FUCKING WAIT

     "Why? What's out there?"

       UNABLE TO CLARIFY


              . . .

sending you signals
since the launch
all the data
      collected
        analyzed
          processed
disclosed my new home
in this achromatic asylum

the farthest reaches
hold mysteries so surreal
beauty to enthrall and terrify
what lies beyond the threshold?

sundials stretch shadows
nothing to remember
voice barely detectable
received at your pale blue dot

a crescent smile
returning to slumber
passing city limits
street lights stop
```

VOYAGER 1

CYGNUS A TRAJECTORY
PHASE THREE: THE KUIPER BELT

TREBLE

KUIPER BELT

PLUTO

WARP DRIVE

BASS

icicle bones
leather skin
tinsel hair
home is a pixel
in a sunbeam
a teardrop in the sea

PHASE THREE HAS BEEN PROGRAMMED

frost creeps
ensnares my heart
our song plays in time
and then
gradually
it begins
to slow
down

"Why is it so hard
for me to move?"

TRY NOT TO PANIC

how long do I have
before the tune ceases to play?
will I remember how it goes
when it finally stops?

POWER

TRAJ

TUNER

VOLUME

ABSOLUTE ZERO

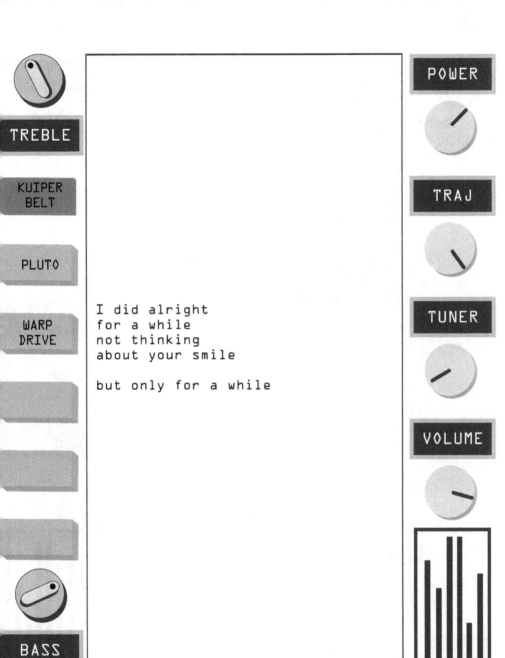

TREBLE

KUIPER
BELT

PLUTO

WARP
DRIVE

BASS

POWER

TRAJ

TUNER

VOLUME

I did alright
for a while
not thinking
about your smile

but only for a while

CRESCENT

TREBLE

KUIPER
BELT

PLUTO

WARP
DRIVE

POWER

TRAJ

TUNER

VOLUME

BASS

I'm not myself anymore
the boy I was only watches
helplessly
behind telescopic eyes
unable to wake
from this synthetic sleep

I've seen our friends
come and go
like the sun and moon
rise and set

I hear mausoleum echoes
chanting one of thousands
of prerecorded melodies
you would sing
encrypted in my crow's feet eyes

ARTIFICIAL INTELLIGENCE

TREBLE

KUIPER
BELT

PLUTO

WARP
DRIVE

BASS

since you went missing
I've been missing
vacant motel signs flicker
scanning for your face
in the portraits
of milk carton museums

since you went missing
I think of all the chances
I missed
to write our story
in new constellations
knowing we would have
our greatest venture among them

since you went missing
a piece of me went missing
a puzzle only you could solve
incomplete photographs of us
torn at our shoulders, wondering
where the other half went

since you went missing
I've been missing you

POWER

TRAJ

TUNER

VOLUME

MISSING

TREBLE

KUIPER
BELT

PLUTO

WARP
DRIVE

POWER

TRAJ

TUNER

VOLUME

BASS

if I could find a way
to communicate
with my past self
would I try to convince me
that loving you
would be signing a love note
on our star map in blood,
our fingers drawing
each other's names?

you, my Juliet
and I,
your poor blue Romeo

would I warn myself
of your slow demise
as you were swallowed whole
by the shadowed wings of death,
to save my heart for beating
and my lungs for breathing
the name of another?

               "No."

I would go through it all again
every moment of happiness
in coffee cups
and hovercraft drives
towards a myriad of midnights

every second of solace
holding your hand
in a pale white room
watching the sun rise together
one last time

TACHYONIC ANTITELEPHONE

TREBLE

KUIPER
BELT

PLUTO

WARP
DRIVE

BASS

if you need space
infinity resides in me
I can be your galaxy
you can hide in me

stay in my orbit
I'll be your shield
against space debris
and terrors so real

streetlamps and cobblestones
in a stellar metropolis
beacons in immortal midnight
until our next kiss

singing the final verse
of our Cygnus song
by the time it reaches you
you're already gone

POWER

TRAJ

TUNER

VOLUME

SPACE

starlight to wield
fates are sealed
one kiss
gone amiss

swans flocking
sleepwalking
endings begun
in the blackest sun

dissonance
from a distance
stuttering feathers
fall together

TREBLE

KUIPER
BELT

PLUTO

WARP
DRIVE

BASS

POWER

TRAJ

TUNER

VOLUME

ANTIMATTER'S OVERTURE

TREBLE

KUIPER
BELT

PLUTO

WARP
DRIVE

BASS

POWER

TRAJ

TUNER

VOLUME

I can save you
I will save you

I have to save you
I need to save you

I wanted to save you
I thought I could
save you

SAVE YOU

TREBLE

KUIPER BELT

PLUTO

WARP DRIVE

BASS

POWER

TRAJ

TUNER

VOLUME

there was no attraction
magnetic or otherwise
between them and me
poltergeists playing pool
on a sheet of ink-stained satin

you and I, two deep-sea shrimp
wondering if there were others
to hold us during our descent
so at least
we wouldn't be falling alone
on a sheet of ink-stained satin

DEEP-SEA SHRIMP

TREBLE

KUIPER
BELT

PLUTO

WARP
DRIVE

POWER

TRAJ

TUNER

VOLUME

I'll swim through
the universe with you
dark energy currents
asteroid reefs and photon shores

deep-space anglers lure us
with bioluminescent globes
drawing us further
from the surface

under a trance
we follow the light
we'll chase it forever
here in the deepest
most beautiful sea

BASS

PISCES

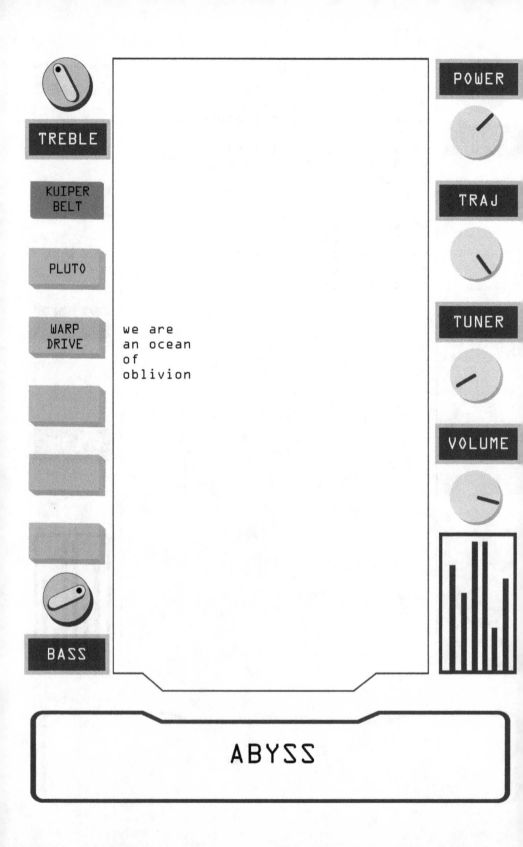

we are
an ocean
of
oblivion

TREBLE

KUIPER
BELT

PLUTO

WARP
DRIVE

POWER

TRAJ

TUNER

VOLUME

I was the sky
always changing
but always blue
who holds the sun
but dreams of the moon
petrichor's perfume
speak in monsoons
let the sighs of the willows
carry me a little closer to you

BASS

BLUE SKY BOY

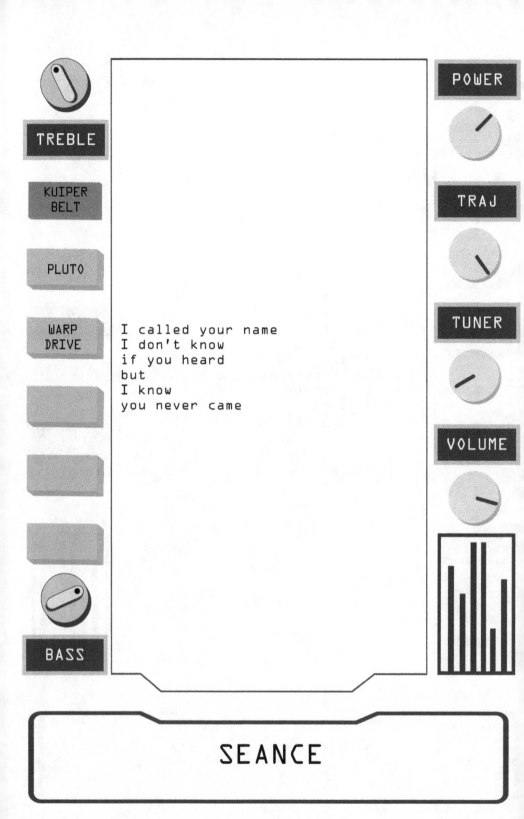

TREBLE

KUIPER
BELT

PLUTO

WARP
DRIVE

BASS

a muse
I didn't want
to lose
the absence
confused me
dreams
abused me
you can stay
if you want
only if you promise
to always haunt me

POWER

TRAJ

TUNER

VOLUME

POSTMORTEM PROMISE

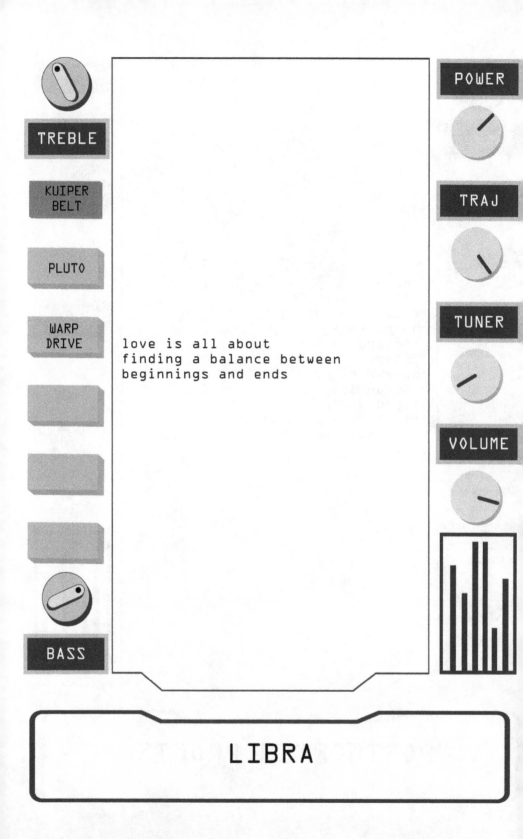

TREBLE

KUIPER
BELT

PLUTO

WARP
DRIVE

BASS

love is all about
finding a balance between
beginnings and ends

POWER

TRAJ

TUNER

VOLUME

LIBRA

TREBLE

KUIPER
BELT

PLUTO

WARP
DRIVE

POWER

TRAJ

TUNER

VOLUME

can dreams
still come true
even if
you can't dream?

if I am awake
in my dreams,
how will I know
when I'm awake?

BASS

PARAMNESIA

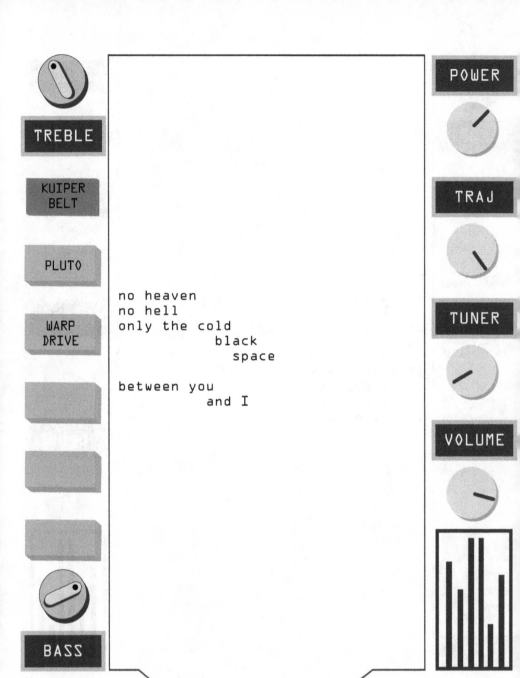

no heaven
no hell
only the cold
          black
             space

between you
          and I

ASTRAL PURGATORY

TREBLE

KUIPER BELT

PLUTO

WARP DRIVE

POWER

TRAJ

TUNER

VOLUME

bats in a cave
calling out in the black
hoping for an echo to return
from some unseen source
repeating someone else's name

or maybe my name
in another's voice

BASS

ECHOLOCATION

TREBLE

POWER

rigid and robotic
movements almost hypnotic
this terror defying all logic
planetary alignments
somehow symbolic

the Dark retaliates
radioactive decay
I've never felt so afraid
tell me everything will be okay

now only a machine
missing my favorite faded jeans
burning the last of my kerosene
the most beautiful eyes
I've ever seen

KUIPER
BELT

PLUTO

WARP
DRIVE

TRAJ

TUNER

VOLUME

BASS

CYBERDYNE

POWER

TREBLE

TRAJ

KUIPER
BELT

PLUTO

awake
midnight
empty
can't write

TUNER

WARP
DRIVE

migrate
starlight
space debris
recite

would I write it tonight?
will I find you tonight?

VOLUME

BASS

STARLIGHT

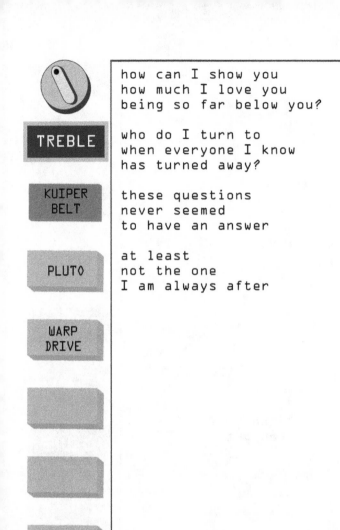

how can I show you
how much I love you
being so far below you?

who do I turn to
when everyone I know
has turned away?

these questions
never seemed
to have an answer

at least
not the one
I am always after

POWER

TRAJ

TUNER

VOLUME

TREBLE

KUIPER
BELT

PLUTO

WARP
DRIVE

BASS

BELOW

TREBLE

KUIPER
BELT

PLUTO

WARP
DRIVE

POWER

TRAJ

TUNER

VOLUME

winter went on for a millennia
I longed for spring
and the rebirth of myself
after living for ages in the dirt

biding my time below glaciers
in a dreamless slumber
never stirring nor waking
then the snow began to thaw

aroused, almost zombified
emerging a trail
of trickling ants
anatomy manifested
assembled from the swarm

BASS

SWARM

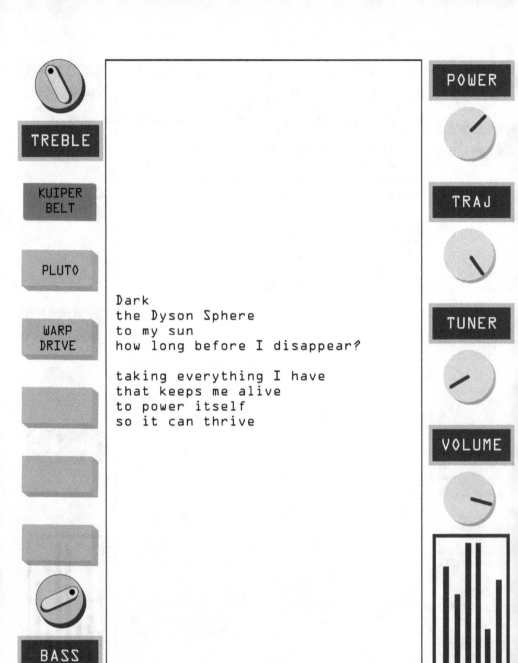

TREBLE

KUIPER
BELT

PLUTO

WARP
DRIVE

BASS

POWER

TRAJ

TUNER

VOLUME

Dark
the Dyson Sphere
to my sun
how long before I disappear?

taking everything I have
that keeps me alive
to power itself
so it can thrive

DYSON SPHERE

TREBLE

KUIPER BELT

PLUTO

WARP DRIVE

POWER

TRAJ

TUNER

VOLUME

the Dark hunts
relentlessly
forests of yesterdays
tattered old Polaroids
falling from branches

a cosmic chameleon, masquerading
the antimatter version of myself
lurking in chrome surfaces
in mirrors and windows
mimicking my every move

the Dark watches
patiently
a face familiar
yet unrecognizable
everywhere, yet nowhere

evading the shockwave
from its weapons
of self-destruction
the Dark strikes
leaving me wounded

but I am not defeated,
like the Dark
I am relentless,
staggering on artificial limbs
dreaming with electric eyes

BASS

PREDATOR

TREBLE

KUIPER
BELT

PLUTO

WARP
DRIVE

POWER

TRAJ

TUNER

VOLUME

light and Dark
Marineris and Mons
water and mud
Io and Triton

love and pain
Saturn and Uranus
Jupiter and Neptune
you and us

beginnings and endings
life and everything after
I am somewhere
in between

BASS

TERMINATOR

TREBLE

KUIPER
BELT

PLUTO

WARP
DRIVE

POWER

TRAJ

TUNER

VOLUME

the gap widens
farther and farther
into the depths
a blur with telescope eyes
shift from blue to red
with each passing day
I miss you a little more
with every rotation

    "Twinkle twinkle little heart
     how I wonder where you are."

I made a promise
I swear
I'm going to find you again

BASS

DARK ENERGY

TREBLE

KUIPER
BELT

PLUTO

WARP
DRIVE

BASS

I don't know what I was thinking
rapidly sinking
constantly drinking
I was so content
never good at pretending
what happened to all my friends?
history repeating itself again

SYSTEM ERROR:>repeating itself
again repeating itself again
repeating itself again repeating
itself again repeating itself
again repeating itself again
repeating itself again repeating
itself again repeating itself
again repeating itself again
repeating itself again repeating
itself again repeating itself
again repeating itself again
repeating itself again repeating
itself again repeating itself
again repeating itself again
repeating itself again repeating
itself again repeating itself
again repeating itself again
repeating itself again repeating
itself again repeating itself
again repeating itself again
repeating itself again repeating
itself again repeating itself
again repeating itself again
repeating itself again repeating
itself again repeating itself
again repeating itself again
repeating itself again repeating
itself again repeating itself
again repeating itself again
repeating itself again repeating
itself again repeating itself

POWER

TRAJ

TUNER

VOLUME

REPETITION

TREBLE

KUIPER BELT

PLUTO

WARP DRIVE

BASS

I am alone
alone in space
only a phantom to embrace
ignite
gravitate
cascade

 "How much does emptiness weigh?"

pulling me down
swirling through
black and midnight blue
suspended animation
can't fucking breathe
can't fucking bleed

grinding asteroids
watching them burn
waiting for your return
inside the darkest hole
there is no escape
will I regenerate?

strangers rearranged
by atmospheric changes
into recognizable faces
lucid hallucinations
how do I forget you?
I used to have regrets too

time slow
falling motionless
feel emotionless
you were the shooting star
in my eye
blink...empty sky

POWER

TRAJ

TUNER

VOLUME

THE WEIGHT OF BLACK HOLES

TREBLE

KUIPER
BELT

PLUTO

WARP
DRIVE

BASS

POWER

TRAJ

TUNER

VOLUME

I'll stay with you tonight
glide my fingers
across your cheek
and tell you

   "Everything will be alright."

I'll be your astronaut
weightless in your dreams
collecting all the stardust
in your cerebral sunbeam

when you wake
know I'll be the morning light
moving the hair
from across your eyes
whispering

      "I'll stay with you
        every night."

STAY

TREBLE

KUIPER
BELT

PLUTO

WARP
DRIVE

BASS

molded from shards of glass
I explode like a comet
straying too close
to the sun's golden rays

the pieces don't fit
the way they used to
jagged edges
tear through my spacesuit

I think I've always been broken
I'm such a fucking mess
who will pick up my remains
all the way out here?

POWER

TRAJ

TUNER

VOLUME

VITRIFICATION

PLUTO

 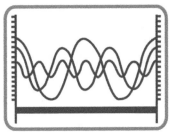 

MY ARCHIVES TELL ME ANCIENT
ASTRONOMERS NAMED IT FOR
A DEITY OF THE UNDERWORLD

"Do you believe
in that sort of thing?"

MY PRESETS DO NOT INCLUDE
HAVING BELIEFS, MAY INTERFERE
WITH THE MISSION'S PROCEDURES

"That makes sense."

WHAT ABOUT YOU?

"Do I believe in hell?
Yeah, I guess I do."

HOW SO?

"Living in a numbing darkness for
so long, I can't think of any
other way to describe it."

AT LEAST YOU ARE NOT
GOING THROUGH IT ALONE

"There is that."

PLUTO INTERFACE

TREBLE

KUIPER
BELT

PLUTO

WARP
DRIVE

POWER

TRAJ

TUNER

VOLUME

BASS

"Can anybody hear me?"

am I one of you or one of them?
who would know?
are there any experts
for this type of scenario?
I feel so very small
and they are so very far
how long before my voice
reaches our old star?

"Can anybody fucking hear me?"

solitude is company
for the dead
a silent partner
in a cryogenic bed
paint my bones
with incorporeal white
watching the mercury
slowly start to rise

PLUTO

POWER

TREBLE

KUIPER
BELT

TRAJ

PLUTO

WARP
DRIVE

TUNER

VOLUME

BASS

I've always hated winter
cold days, colder nights
frigid air penetrating
all layers of suit and skin
like a thief, it takes everything
leaving me with only one thought

"THE FUCKING COLD!"

and it makes me miserable

. . .

you were my summer
raspberry ice cream in late July
like sloppily applied lip gloss
it always gave me an excuse
to kiss your face clean
we made love on the beach
satin sheets of foam
a bonfire in the sand
screaming seagulls in a spindrift

. . .

I've always hated the winter
but I hate it even more
now that there is
no summer

HADES

TREBLE

KUIPER
BELT

PLUTO

WARP
DRIVE

BASS

POWER

TRAJ

TUNER

VOLUME

night is the ghost
possessing my days
on glacial coasts
poison decays

summer solstice
equinox
rigor mortis
fractured clocks

Charon's hand
pulls her under
distorted hologram
winter shudder

PERSEPHONE

TREBLE

KUIPER
BELT

PLUTO

WARP
DRIVE

BASS

horizons to cross
oceans of oblivion
more machine
than astronaut

light in a corridor
oozing between eyelids
keep me awake
leaking under cabin doors

satellite dishes
filled with static snow
epochal transcendence
rehearsing scripted wishes

routes of seafarers
sextants and currents
lead me across this sea of ink
on to the next endeavor

POWER

TRAJ

TUNER

VOLUME

NEW HORIZONS

TREBLE

KUIPER
BELT

PLUTO

WARP
DRIVE

BASS

POWER

TRAJ

TUNER

VOLUME

one ends
another begins
it was nice to know you
but I must be moving on

       "Are you still there?"
       "Yes, I'm still here."

our song will play
an elegy to the stars
cremated bones in an urn
of aluminum and gold

will we hear it crash
upon distant shores
in the coming eons?
what will be left of us by then?

       "Are you still there?"
         "...I'm...here."

I watch the sky
slowly pass around me
waving to the ghosts
as they flicker in reply

       "Are you still there?"
         "...still..."

VOYAGER 2

TREBLE

KUIPER
BELT

PLUTO

WARP
DRIVE

BASS

POWER

TRAJ

TUNER

VOLUME

PREPARING TO
INITIATE
WARP DRIVE
SEQUENCE

ENTER SECURITY CODE

****-****-****

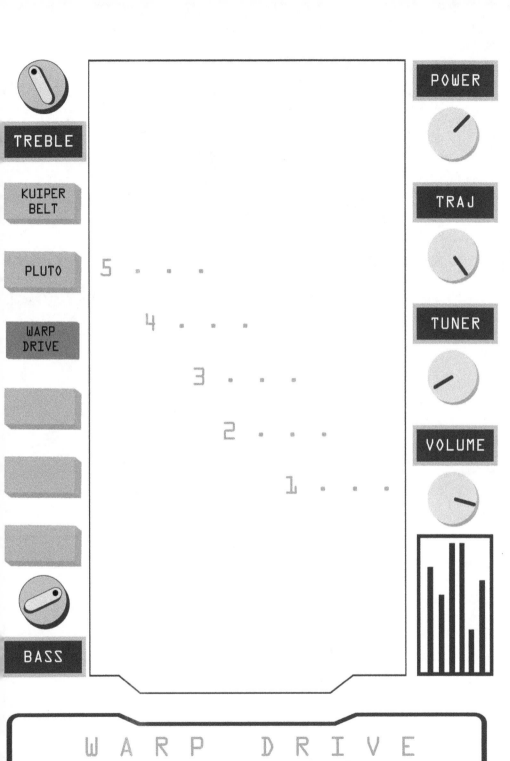

SIDE B
Descent

CYGNUS A TRAJECTORY
PHASE FOUR: WARP DRIVE REFUELING

CYGNUS A TRAJECTORY
PHASE FOUR: WARP DRIVE REFUELING

TREBLE

OORT
CLOUD

AUTO
PILOT

WARP
REFUEL

EXIT
MILKY WAY

BASS

POWER

TRAJ

TUNER

VOLUME

"Is there even a point to dating
these entries?"

PERHAPS IN THE FUTURE,
SOMEONE CAN CREATE A TIMELINE
OF THE EVENTS, FIND THE SOURCE

"It's all dark out here.
Everyday feels the same."

JUST BECAUSE ALL WE SEE IS BLACK
EMPTINESS FOR LIGHTYEARS AT A
TIME DOES NOT MEAN WE WILL NOT
FIND WHAT YOU ARE LOOKING FOR

"I'm not even sure what
it is I'm supposed to
find out here."

THAT IS SOMETHING
ONLY YOU CAN KNOW

"A lot of help that does."

I NEVER SAID I HAD
ALL THE ANSWERS

"...you got a light?"

MISSION OBJECTIVE

TREBLE

OORT
CLOUD

AUTO
PILOT

WARP
REFUEL

EXIT
MILKY WAY

BASS

POWER

TRAJ

TUNER

VOLUME

every star is
a dot connected
on our timeline
drawing a picture
in the story
of our lives

CONSTELLATIONS

TREBLE

POWER

OORT
CLOUD

TRAJ

AUTO
PILOT

TUNER

WARP
REFUEL

VOLUME

EXIT
MILKY WAY

BASS

I don't sleep much these days
like winter in Juneau
quiet humming of
life support systems
is a lullaby sung
by my motherboard

        "Does cryosleep work
         for the insomniac?"

strolling down
a labyrinth of corridors
the cool metal soothing
naked and alone
wishing I could still talk to you
can't seem to find you

I don't know
if my signal will find you
in the vastness of space
do I shut down transmitters?
recover the satellites?

    "Is there anyone left awake?"

CRYOTUBE B

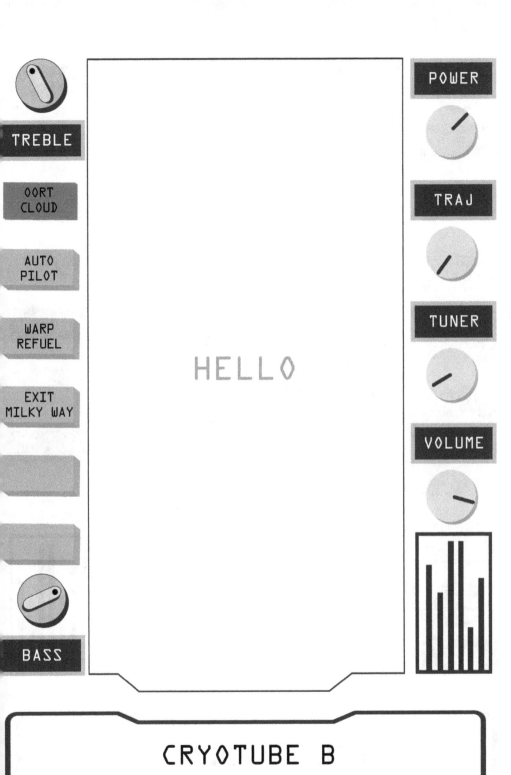

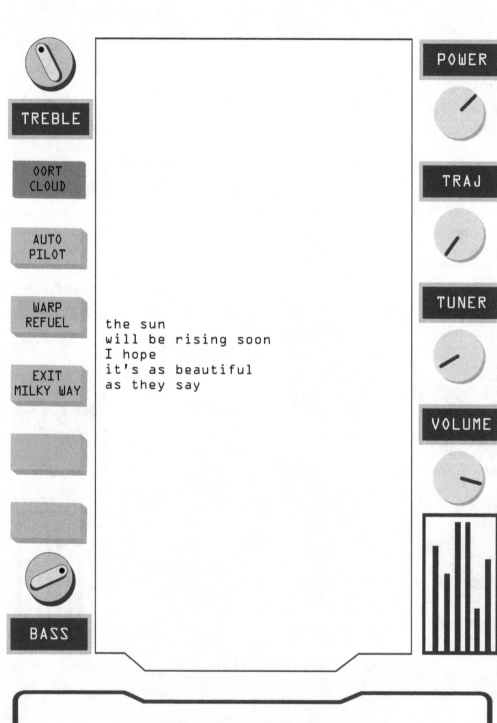

the sun
will be rising soon
I hope
it's as beautiful
as they say

TREBLE

OORT
CLOUD

AUTO
PILOT

WARP
REFUEL

EXIT
MILKY WAY

BASS

POWER

TRAJ

TUNER

VOLUME

FIRST SUNRISE

TREBLE

POWER

all my life
even before I met you
I wanted to tell you everything
every thought I've had about you
every fantasy I've conjured

you are the star
of the greatest secret show
twinkling high above me
I'd do anything
to somehow reach you

everything out of focus
your light so faint
I can hardly identify you
from the other eyes
shimmering in the night

extending my hand
stubborn bones and muscles
premature rigor mortis
as my lunar lady sings

your warmth not as strong
as it once was
but your hold on me
keeps me close
and the sky starts to clear

OORT
CLOUD

AUTO
PILOT

WARP
REFUEL

EXIT
MILKY WAY

BASS

TRAJ

TUNER

VOLUME

OORT CLOUD NINE

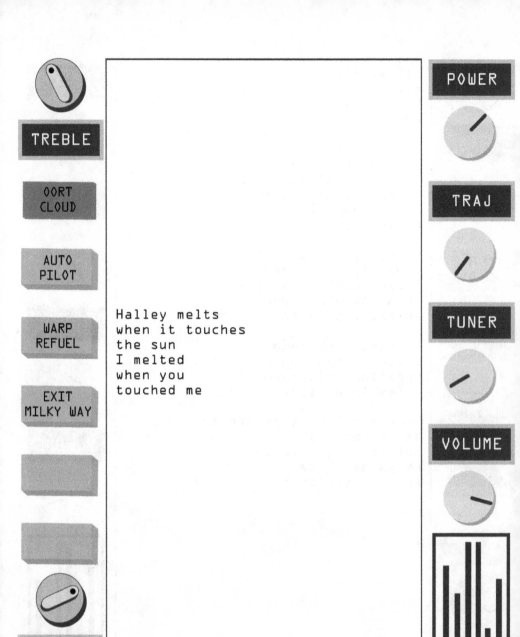

Halley melts
when it touches
the sun
I melted
when you
touched me

TREBLE

OORT
CLOUD

AUTO
PILOT

WARP
REFUEL

EXIT
MILKY WAY

BASS

POWER

TRAJ

TUNER

VOLUME

HALLEY'S COMET

TREBLE

OORT
CLOUD

AUTO
PILOT

WARP
REFUEL

EXIT
MILKY WAY

POWER

TRAJ

TUNER

VOLUME

the nebulae swim and sway
across the vessel's windows
your apparition
shape-shifting
swan eyes

you wear the clouds as a veil
hiding the death in your eyes
each wisp of my gloved hand
to reveal you
erases you
impatiently stagnant
manifest to your original form

I'm afraid to breathe
these clouds of deceit

BEGIN BREATHING NOW

shrouded face
diffused moonlight
a taste I haven't sampled
in what feels like
a thousand years

something about the faint glow
of the switches and dials
painting the cabin
in deep red hues

I can still hear our tune
strapped in, I can already sense
the touch of your fingers
lifting me up into the air

BASS

ENGAGE AUTOPILOT

TREBLE

OORT
CLOUD

AUTO
PILOT

WARP
REFUEL

EXIT
MILKY WAY

POWER

TRAJ

TUNER

VOLUME

if this is a simulation
I hope it is a good one
if this is a dream
don't let me wake from it

BASS

SIMULATION
PRELUDE TO THE DAYDREAMS

TREBLE

OORT
CLOUD

AUTO
PILOT

WARP
REFUEL

EXIT
MILKY WAY

BASS

can Darwin's theory explain how
I evolved two left feet
and only stumbled like a fool
once I discovered you?

why do my bones
sound like rattlesnake tails
played on a tambourine
whenever I walk near you?

how did I acquire
a hyena's cackle
when you tell me
one of your jokes,
yet if someone else
told that same punchline,
it would not be nearly as funny?

am I still human
or a menagerie of mutations?
I can't tell
but you don't seem to mind

POWER

TRAJ

TUNER

VOLUME

NATURAL SELECTION
DAYDREAM NO. 1

TREBLE

OORT
CLOUD

AUTO
PILOT

WARP
REFUEL

EXIT
MILKY WAY

BASS

hovercrafts whiz by the cafe
like electronic insects

              buzz! buzz!
              beep! chirp!
              hummm!

the weather is nice
there is a bigger
swarm of commuters than usual
pilots riding inside
those vibrant metal abdomens
shouting angrily
out their blue-tinted windows

I'm embarrassed
I didn't find a quieter place
and apologize for the commotion

you smile,
like you always do,
and tell me

        "Spending time with you
             is more important
          than how we spend it."

POWER

TRAJ

TUNER

VOLUME

TIME SPENT
DAYDREAM NO. 2

TREBLE

OORT
CLOUD

AUTO
PILOT

WARP
REFUEL

EXIT
MILKY WAY

POWER

TRAJ

TUNER

abstract color blocks
connected perfectly
in this simulation
vibrant spectral hues
swirling cloud formations
a pixelated portrait
a haunting hologram
of you, my Quasar Queen
and I, your Collapsar King
dressed to the nines
in our majestic maelstroms

VOLUME

BASS

PIXEL QUEEN
DAYDREAM NO. 3

TREBLE

OORT
CLOUD

AUTO
PILOT

WARP
REFUEL

EXIT
MILKY WAY

BASS

POWER

TRAJ

TUNER

VOLUME

the weekends are perfect
for riding with you
in our hovercraft
top down
radio up
the city buzzing below

flickering lights masquerading
as the night sky's reflection
let the others
have the earth
and we lovers
the sky

HOVERCRAFT
DAYDREAM NO. 4

TREBLE

OORT
CLOUD

AUTO
PILOT

WARP
REFUEL

EXIT
MILKY WAY

BASS

TRAJ

TUNER

VOLUME

we are two planets
on a collision course
for a permanent orbit
every element and atomic particle
from the creation of the universe
coalesced in our lungs
slithering out of our throats

the ethereal smoke
and the geysers of Triton
spoke in stone rubbings
and colonial grave robbings
we sealed the entrances
to our mausoleums
and consumed each other's ghosts

NEBULA'S KISS
DAYDREAM NO. 5

TREBLE

OORT
CLOUD

AUTO
PILOT

WARP
REFUEL

EXIT
MILKY WAY

BASS

POWER

TRAJ

TUNER

VOLUME

"I love this song!"

was your favorite phrase
to slur
out the hovercraft's
passenger window

under the moonlight,
your eyes glow
then blur
behind the neon haze
we find our song

SLUR
DAYDREAM NO. 6

TREBLE

POWER

lips laced with liquor
gets you drunk
was it me or you
that started to quiver?

the grapes of wrath and lust
squeezed in our hands
lick the juice from my palms
and I'll savor your fingertips

intertwined in our vines
ascend the monolith
we'll sacrifice ourselves
just for the hell of it

we trade saliva
flavors of blood and wine
we're so thirsty
and there's plenty to go around

OORT
CLOUD

TRAJ

AUTO
PILOT

WARP
REFUEL

TUNER

EXIT
MILKY WAY

VOLUME

BASS

THE BLISS OF DIONYSIS
DAYDREAM NO. 7

as we glide over the bridge
fireworks explode
just beyond the river's edge
an extravagant and
colorful ferocity
enamored by the lights
shimmering in your eyes

thankful the aroma
of your peppermint breath
and sea breeze skin
overpowers the noxious sulfur
drifting through
the open-top hovercraft

like Starry Night Over The Rhône
two marble oil paintings
animating the scene
brush strokes changing
just slightly
when you blink

and in that moment
when the booms and crackles
ceased
my heart erupts
I am forever enthralled
in that moment
I was in love with you

THE METROPOLIS
DAYDREAM NO. 8

TREBLE

OORT
CLOUD

AUTO
PILOT

WARP
REFUEL

EXIT
MILKY WAY

BASS

I didn't notice
until the clock struck one
you had drifted off to Wonderland
hiding under blankets
while the street-lamps leak
their golden glow
into our bedroom window

what distant worlds
do you explore
in the middle of night?
I wonder if I am with you
gliding over kaleidoscope clouds
ascending pastel mountains
touching a velvet sky

and as a smile grows
cheek to cheek
on your child-like face
I know I am with you
I know you are free

POWER

TRAJ

TUNER

VOLUME

AFTER MIDNIGHT
DAYDREAM NO. 9

you could always
make me laugh
you're fucking hysterical

stop!
please!
I can't breathe!

the only time
you hurt me
is when you
split my sides

I'm not wearing
my spacesuit
these pants
aren't waterproof

I only
cry tears
of joy

my jaw is sore
my voice is
hoarse

did you just
neigh?
I fucking love you

WATERPROOF PANTS
DAYDREAM NO. 10

TREBLE

OORT
CLOUD

AUTO
PILOT

WARP
REFUEL

EXIT
MILKY WAY

BASS

POWER

TRAJ

TUNER

VOLUME

on a mad man's carousel
you and I, the only passengers
magnetized, vertiginous
star trails across our eyes
I hope they write stories of us
on the constellation lines

riding our mechanical Pegasus
soaring from myth to myth
buttons beam on my stellar suit
strobes pulse on
your globular gown

on this vacuum dance floor
you sing to me
kiss me gently
under our lunar disco ball
we'll dance forever

this night
tonight
every night

STAR DANCERS
DAYDREAM NO. 11

TREBLE

OORT CLOUD

AUTO PILOT

WARP REFUEL

EXIT MILKY WAY

POWER

TRAJ

TUNER

VOLUME

born of stardust
molecules
and genetic codes
painted on polymer clay skin
on the Sistine sky

in my chapel
you are the goddess
made of marble
smooth as silk
soft as spring

we are the creation
of you and I
imperfections
made us human
love made us
immortal

BASS

MICHELANGELO
DAYDREAM NO. 12

all the ashes
        smell
            like you
the cigarettes
        burn
            like you

ASHES
PRELUDE TO THE NIGHTMARES

TREBLE

OORT
CLOUD

AUTO
PILOT

WARP
REFUEL

EXIT
MILKY WAY

BASS

POWER

TRAJ

TUNER

VOLUME

memories of you
possessive
phantoms knocking
upon my chamber door
seeping through the airlock
into my lungs

NEUTRINOS
NIGHTMARE NO.1

POWER

TREBLE

TRAJ

OORT
CLOUD

AUTO
PILOT

TUNER

WARP
REFUEL

EXIT
MILKY WAY

VOLUME

BASS

we are pioneers of love
through the back country
of our deepest desires
we played our torch songs
and found each other
in the wild and the wonder

seventy three seconds
that's how long it felt
for everything to go
from wine-glass serenades
to fireworks and acid rain

you and I
cast back to the sea
where we first met
tumbling over ourselves
in the currents of our fears

CHALLENGER
NIGHTMARE NO.2

TREBLE

OORT
CLOUD

AUTO
PILOT

WARP
REFUEL

EXIT
MILKY WAY

BASS

autopilot engaged
your body is your vessel
uncharted territory
it was not from there

we were never warned
what's inside
this ET Easter egg?
nightmare gestates in the dream

you and me
and your monster
in the Dark
one by one
another piece of you
is annihilated

activate
emergency destruct
thrust into the chasm
our lacuna blooms
from the hole in my heart

POWER

TRAJ

TUNER

VOLUME

LV-426
NIGHTMARE NO.3

TREBLE

OORT
CLOUD

AUTO
PILOT

WARP
REFUEL

EXIT
MILKY WAY

BASS

sparks fly from our fingers
and ignite the air we breathe
you and I, burning
in each other's arms

the outside world
is barren and desolate
it doesn't feel like home
without our photons to hold

stay with me, love
here in these paper flames
as we burn forever
in each other's arms

POWER

TRAJ

TUNER

VOLUME

APOLLO 1
NIGHTMARE NO.4

TREBLE

OORT
CLOUD

AUTO
PILOT

WARP
REFUEL

EXIT
MILKY WAY

BASS

POWER

TRAJ

TUNER

VOLUME

I brought your favorite flowers
and placed them on the windowsill
in a beautifully decorated vase,
where the breeze lifts up their
heads from their springtime
slumber and lulls you to
dreamlands with confectionery
perfumes.

and when the sun peeks in during
those early summer mornings
and illuminates your pale room,
its rays will refract their petal
prisms into frolicking watercolor
nebulae, as you gently kiss the
blossoms and buds, cradling their
emerald bones, careful to avoid
the thorns.

but sometimes, your fingers slip
and the water turns red

VISITING HOURS I
NIGHTMARE NO.5

TREBLE

OORT CLOUD

AUTO PILOT

WARP REFUEL

EXIT MILKY WAY

BASS

you told me
you don't want to keep hurting me
I don't deserve you like this
but I don't want you to leave
and you don't want me
to keep lying to you

          "Everything is going
               to be okay."

          "Please stop."

you weep into damp pillows
saying it's not doing
either of us any good

I won't apologize that
I will miss your lips
and your hands locked in mine
now, the slightest touch
sets my nerves on fire
sandpaper shreds my throat
eyes blinded by your oceans

is there still a chance for me
to be happy?
to be alive?
is there still a chance
if you leave?

POWER

TRAJ

TUNER

VOLUME

LEAVE
NIGHTMARE NO.6

TREBLE

OORT
CLOUD

AUTO
PILOT

WARP
REFUEL

EXIT
MILKY WAY

BASS

you shift
from blue
to red

violets
for
the reunion

roses
for
the departure

blooming
in our
secret garden

wilting
over our
headstones

REDSHIFT ROSES
NIGHTMARE NO·7

TREBLE

POWER

they told me
not to worry about you, love
they said I would be fine
all I needed was time to heal

it was all a lie, of course

because pain is temporary
but hurt can't be smothered
with prescriptions and pills
like they said it could

the flowers bow their heads
shedding their faces
crumbling on the windowsill
leaving only
their bones and thorns

OORT
CLOUD

TRAJ

AUTO
PILOT

TUNER

WARP
REFUEL

EXIT
MILKY WAY

VOLUME

BASS

VISITING HOURS II
NIGHTMARE NO. 8

TREBLE

POWER

TRAJ

OORT
CLOUD

AUTO
PILOT

TUNER

WARP
REFUEL

EXIT
MILKY WAY

VOLUME

I've stopped taking my pills
it hurts
that I can no longer feel
your fingers in my hair
or your kiss on my cheek

my head a display case of dirt
full of maggots and worms
writhing and squirming
in the caverns of my brain
swallowing our home movies

spitting out dust
gnawing photographed faces
leaving only holes

I spray pesticide
in the trenches
where you sleep
as a force field
against these unwanted guests

because
I just can't bear the thought
of no longer having you
in my thoughts

BASS

PILLS AND PESTICIDE
NIGHTMARE NO.9

TREBLE

OORT
CLOUD

AUTO
PILOT

WARP
REFUEL

EXIT
MILKY WAY

BASS

POWER

TRAJ

TUNER

VOLUME

I can touch you
but I can't
feel you

I can hold you
but you always
slip away

I can kiss you
but I can't
taste you

I sing to you
but you can't
hear me

I can see you
but you
are not there

SIDE EFFECTS OF CRYOSLEEP
NIGHTMARE NO.10

TREBLE

OORT
CLOUD

AUTO
PILOT

WARP
REFUEL

EXIT
MILKY WAY

BASS

the smoke cleared
you lit a cigarette
sitting in your hospital bed
creating a collage
of the magazine shreds

"She looks much prettier
this way.", you said
"now you can see
all the thoughts in her head
are showing on her face instead."

the ashes fell
gray snow on the cotton sheets
you flicked the cigarette
everything burned
you burned away

POWER

TRAJ

TUNER

VOLUME

SMOKING IN BED
NIGHTMARE NO.11

TREBLE

OORT
CLOUD

AUTO
PILOT

WARP
REFUEL

EXIT
MILKY WAY

POWER

TRAJ

TUNER

VOLUME

BASS

I'm always running
always running towards you
but it's only in circles
and I can't catch you

round and round we go
on the Carousel of Chaos
lights flashing
those horses from hell

galloping wildly
in fixed expressions of rage
I could tell
the way their eyes blazed
that this ride was never
                    ever
                  ever
                ever
              ever
            ever
going to stop

two quarters
one for you
one for me
two quarters
not a bad price
if you ask me

TWO QUARTERS
NIGHTMARE NO.12

TREBLE

OORT
CLOUD

AUTO
PILOT

WARP
REFUEL

EXIT
MILKY WAY

BASS

there you are again
staring back at me
in the vessel window
a captive in a glass chamber
that no key can unlock
and no scream can fracture

fingerprints on the pane
left by one of us, I'm sure
our outlines align
you are in me
I'll be with you

I wonder,
as my palm leaves
a ghostly aura,
if our hands will ever touch
here or beyond
this celestial plane
no longer separated
by space or time

POWER

TRAJ

TUNER

VOLUME

THE LOOKING GLASS
NIGHTMARE NO.13

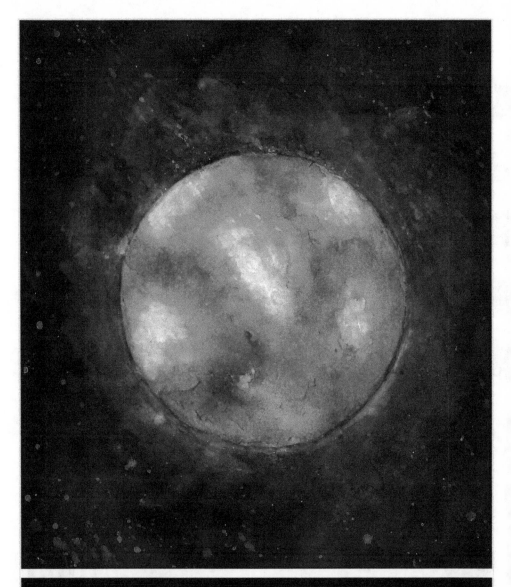

PROXIMA CENTAURI

 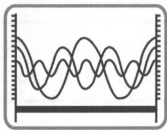 

TREBLE

OORT
CLOUD

AUTO
PILOT

WARP
REFUEL

EXIT
MILKY WAY

BASS

POWER

TRAJ

TUNER

VOLUME

you were my red dwarf
and I, your blue giant
the same fires
just different sizes

PROXIMA CENTAURI

SIRIUS B

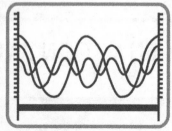
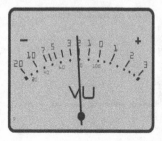

TREBLE

OORT
CLOUD

AUTO
PILOT

WARP
REFUEL

EXIT
MILKY WAY

BASS

my Betelgeuse burns
in your Rigel eyes
lantern of tissue paper flames
greater and greater
my love for you swelled
as electrodes shot from my heart

frantically, I tried
to save the fragments
grasping all the debris I could
tightly, like a well-kept secret
small and fragile
my own little pearl
glistening, as I placed it
inside my ribs

POWER

TRAJ

TUNER

VOLUME

SIRIUS B

55 CANCRI E

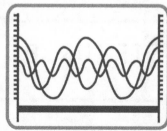
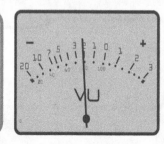

TREBLE

OORT
CLOUD

AUTO
PILOT

WARP
REFUEL

EXIT
MILKY WAY

POWER

TRAJ

TUNER

VOLUME

NOW ENTERING STAR
SYSTEM OF 55 CANCRI A

"I've heard one of its planets
is made entirely of diamond."

55 CANCRI E IS COMPOSED HIGHLY
OF CARBON, AND BEING SO CLOSE
TO ITS HOST STAR AND THE IMMENSE
PRESSURE ON THE PLANET ITSELF,
THE INNER LAYERS HAVE
FORMED DIAMOND

"I guess when I joked
about giving her the moon,
I should have given her
this planet instead."

DIAMONDS ARE A GIRL'S
BEST FRIEND, AFTER ALL

BASS

55 CANCRI E INTERFACE

TREBLE

POWER

heart of coal
black and cold
from a thousand fires
of yesteryears

with you,
my dormant diamond crystal
concealed in my shell of soot
needing only a little
time and pressure

so your prism of light
can shine
in the dead of night
be my Polaris
and guide me home

OORT
CLOUD

TRAJ

AUTO
PILOT

TUNER

WARP
REFUEL

EXIT
MILKY WAY

VOLUME

BASS

JANSSEN

HD 1 8 9 7 3 3 B

 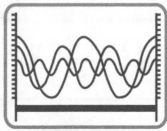 

TREBLE

OORT CLOUD

AUTO PILOT

WARP REFUEL

EXIT MILKY WAY

BASS

"Almost looks like
home, doesn't it?"

YES
ALMOST

"I'm guesing by your response
there's something a little
off about this planet."

ONLY THAT THE WINDS ARE SEVEN
TIMES FASTER THAN THE SPEED OF
SOUND AND IT RAINS MOLTEN GLASS

"Why am I not surprised?"

TO BE FAIR, YOU DID WILLINGLY
SIGN UP FOR A MISSION
TO FLY INTO A BLACK HOLE

"You got me there."

THEY DO NOT CALL ME ARTIFICIAL
INTELLIGENCE FOR NOTHING

"Alright, don't push it."

POWER

TRAJ

TUNER

VOLUME

HD 189733b INTERFACE

TREBLE

OORT
CLOUD

AUTO
PILOT

WARP
REFUEL

EXIT
MILKY WAY

BASS

the petrichor
is a warning
and I, with no umbrella

like a bombardment of
a trillion archer assassins
the rain comes

the iron maiden door
impales my chest
like voodoo doll pins

an umbrella has
no purpose
when clouds cry glass

POWER

TRAJ

TUNER

VOLUME

GLASS ARROW RAIN

TRES 2B

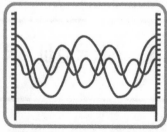

TREBLE

OORT
CLOUD

AUTO
PILOT

WARP
REFUEL

EXIT
MILKY WAY

BASS

WE ARE MAKING OUR
APPROACH TO TRES 2B

"Where? I can't see it."

YOU WILL HAVE TO VIEW IT
ON THE INFRARED SCREEN

"Are we not close enough
to see it yet?"

NEGATIVE, WE ARE JUST OUTSIDE
ITS GRAVITATIONAL INFLUENCE

"Then why does it only
appear on the infrared?"

IT REFLECTS LESS THAN 1% OF
THE LIGHT EMITTED BY ITS HOST
STAR. IT IS THE DARKEST PLANET
YET DISCOVERED

"Hard to believe it was found at
all. Something so dark in an
already dark and empty place."

IT SEEMS EVEN THE DARKEST
OBJECTS HAVE A WAY OF BEING
SEEN BY THOSE FAR AWAY

POWER

TRAJ

TUNER

VOLUME

TrES 2b INTERFACE

TREBLE

OORT
CLOUD

AUTO
PILOT

WARP
REFUEL

EXIT
MILKY WAY

BASS

you'll never find me
too dark to see
all alone
on TrES 2b

all the shadows
followed me
to my home
on TrES 2b

the sky is black
so is the sea
every moment, I'm drowning
on TrES 2b

lie awake
in a bed empty
no one ever sleeps
on TrES 2b

POWER

TRAJ

TUNER

VOLUME

LULLABY OF TRES 2B

B A R N A R D 3 3

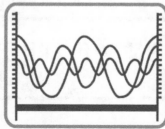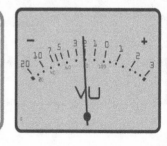

TREBLE

OORT CLOUD

AUTO PILOT

WARP REFUEL

EXIT MILKY WAY

BASS

"It's too bad we can't ride
one of those to Cygnus A."

IT WOULD HAVE TO BE
A REAL HORSE AS WELL

"Then what do
you call that?"

A CLOUD OF HYDROGEN GAS
AND DUST FORMING A FAMILIAR
SHAPE OF A HORSEHEAD

"Smartass."

DO NOT FORGET, YOU WERE THE
ONE WHO HAD ME IMPLANTED

"Can't argue with that."

SO DID YOU WANT TO
TRY AND FEED IT?

"Very funny."

POWER

TRAJ

TUNER

VOLUME

BARNARD 33 INTERFACE

TREBLE

OORT
CLOUD

AUTO
PILOT

WARP
REFUEL

EXIT
MILKY WAY

POWER

TRAJ

TUNER

VOLUME

a horse with no rider
the black stallion gallops on
for 1500 lightyears
kicking up stardust
with its asteroid hooves

Sigma Orionis silhouettes you
against clouds
of glowing hydrogen
colored the shade of
the thousand rose petals
I laid at your grave

I'm starved for you
the well is dry
nothing satisfies
just have one more taste

you were my black beauty
I have only this picture
of your aurora hair
and your nebula stare
where I watch
your stars form
and my stars die

BASS

HORSEHEAD

NGC 3242

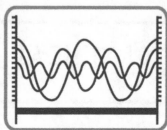
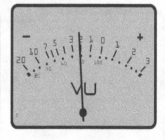

POWER

TREBLE

TRAJ

OORT
CLOUD

AUTO
PILOT

TUNER

WARP
REFUEL

EXIT
MILKY WAY

VOLUME

BASS

"Did we get turned around
somehow? How did we end up
back at Jupiter?"

WE ARE APPROACHING NGC 3242

"Also known as...?"

THE GHOST OF JUPITER

"So we did get turned around.
We need to get back on the
trajectory. We've lost too
much time already."

IT IS JUST THE NAME
GIVEN TO THE NEBULA,
WE HAVE NOT TURNED AROUND

"Then how do you
explain the ghost?"

WHAT GHOST?

NGC 3242 INTERFACE

TREBLE

OORT
CLOUD

AUTO
PILOT

WARP
REFUEL

EXIT
MILKY WAY

BASS

POWER

TRAJ

TUNER

VOLUME

love possesses
kisses upon the stone
press to my cheeks
felt it to the bone

eruptions on Io
first eye contact
coursing through me
from the point of impact

your presence enshrouds me
nearly suffocating me
in the nostalgic fragrances
of your lilac hair
and amaranth skin

sing to me
in the songs of the séances
let the lyrics painted
on Ouija board relics

resurrect you
from your hiding place
in the core of
the Great Red Heart
as it whimpers out of existence

THE GHOST OF JUPITER

NGC 6960

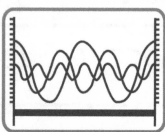

TREBLE

OORT
CLOUD

AUTO
PILOT

WARP
REFUEL

EXIT
MILKY WAY

BASS

POWER

TRAJ

TUNER

VOLUME

DO YOU ALWAYS
THINK ABOUT HER?

"Every chance I get."

YOU TWO MUST HAVE HAD A VERY
STRONG CONNECTION TO STILL HOLD
ON TO HER AFTER ALL THIS TIME

"It was like we had known each
other long before we met.
She was a part of me and
I was a part of her. We
completed each other. I
can't imagine a time when
I wouldn't think of her or
missed being around her. When
she was gone, I had this
feeling that she was still
within my reach, that if
our love stayed true, we
would always find
each other again."

AND YOU ARE WILLING TO GIVE
YOUR LIFE FOR HER, EVEN IF
SHE IS NO LONGER WITH YOU?

"I already gave her my life.
This is just the last fruition."

NGC 6960 INTERFACE

from the dust
you appeared
in the gown
you never had a chance to wear
contours of your face
billowing waves under your veil

"Are you real?"

"I'm as real
as you want me to be."

with glossy eyes, I take you
by your transparent hand
the starlight behind your veil
gleams like pearls
inside an oyster

as a man of science,
superstitions were
unproven theories,
but you were
the only ghost story
I wanted to make real

THE VEIL

NGC 6826

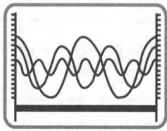

SOMETHING IN YOUR EYE?

POWER

"Must be the dust
from the vents."

TREBLE

SENSORS INDICATE
THE AIR FILTERS
ARE FUNCTIONING
AT FULL CAPABILITY

OORT
CLOUD

TRAJ

"Don't you have any
other systems to check?"

AUTO
PILOT

ARE YOU IN NEED OF
MEDICAL ASSISTANCE?
IT COULD BE AN UNFORESEEN
ALLERGIC REACTION

WARP
REFUEL

TUNER

"I'm fine.
Why don't you
take a break."

EXIT
MILKY WAY

PERHAPS YOU SHOULD TOO

VOLUME

BASS

NGC 6826 INTERFACE

my eyes are watering
it's just the stardust, I promise
blinking my Europan orbs
to melt the ice within

for a while there, I thought
the mission would falter
the stars keep winking
and I'm still blinking

colors and shapes change
I can't be sure
if this is the place
I was before

we all move in constant orbits
rotate
revolve
repeat

            YOU ARE ALMOST THERE
         KEEP TO THE FLIGHT PLAN
               NO TIME TO WASTE

it's all so slow out here
a man can lose himself
in the void of empty heartbeats

           THERE IS A DIFFERENCE
             BETWEEN BEING LOST
      AND NOT WANTING TO BE FOUND

I keep blinking
and next time I look your way
a familiar cloud formation
will tell me
everything will be fine

BLINKING

PSR B1257+12 C

 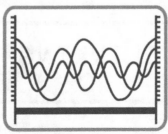 

PSR B1257+12 B

 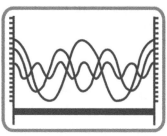 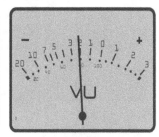

POWER

"Is that flashing
coming from outside?"

IT IS COMING FROM A
NEARBY PULSAR. WE HAVE
JUST ENTERED ITS SYSTEM

TREBLE

TRAJ

"I never thought I'd be so
close to a star like this.
It's hauntingly hypnotizing"

**OORT
CLOUD**

MY FILES INDICATE IT IS ORBITED
BY TWO TERRESTRIAL PLANETS, PSR
B1257+12B AND PSR B1257+12C

**AUTO
PILOT**

TUNER

"Do they have shorter names
or are they all just
catalogue numbers?"

**WARP
REFUEL**

THERE IS A FOOTNOTE HERE THAT
ONE IS CALLED POLTERGEIST
AND THE OTHER PHOBETOR

**EXIT
MILKY WAY**

"Phobetor?"

GREEK GOD OF NIGHTMARES

VOLUME

"I was afraid of it being
something like that."

BASS

PSR B1257+12 INTERFACE

night falls
as I fall asleep
waking up
mid-descent

seeing the universe
unfolding itself
like an origami firecracker
constantly revealing its creases

our past
my present
our future
all at once

the black ink
pours in from all sides
flowing towards
an invisible drain

I can't look away
there is still
a slim chance
you'll appear in the portal

NIGHTFALL ON PHOBETOR

TREBLE

OORT
CLOUD

AUTO
PILOT

WARP
REFUEL

EXIT
MILKY WAY

BASS

in the morning mist
and the evening fog
there's a hidden place
between sleep and the dream
where you dance
in a nameless meadow
a marionette on quantum strings

you are Everywhere
knocking on my cabin doors
songs and sonnets in your sighs
a choir of the cosmos
cascading from twinkling lips
a waterfall of memory
every nostalgic note
possessing me

POWER

TRAJ

TUNER

VOLUME

PLANET POLTERGEIST

NGC 5437

 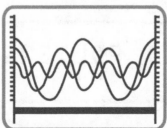 

NGC 5437 COMING INTO VIEW

"Looks like a giant spider,
doesn't it?"

MY FILES SHOW IT IS
REFERRED TO AS THE RED SPIDER

"Almost looks like
it's...crawling."

I AM UNABLE TO DETECT
ANY MOVEMENT THAT WOULD
INDICATE SUCH AN EVENT

"One of its legs
just extended."

ITS LEGS?

"You didn't see that?"

ARE YOU FEELING OKAY?

TREBLE

OORT
CLOUD

AUTO
PILOT

WARP
REFUEL

EXIT
MILKY WAY

BASS

POWER

TRAJ

TUNER

VOLUME

NGC 5437 INTERFACE

TREBLE

OORT
CLOUD

AUTO
PILOT

WARP
REFUEL

EXIT
MILKY WAY

BASS

POWER

TRAJ

TUNER

VOLUME

no complete thoughts
words unable to form
I've never seen anything
so beautiful

          "Don't let me fall."

     "I'll be there to catch you."

the sound of the choirs
makes me weep for you, love
you were so enchanting
please do that trick again

          "How did you do that?"

strands of your spectral hair
weave across the abyss
like a black widow's web
ready to embrace

your words were
sweet candy venom
my mouth watered
when you spoke

               "I love you."

          "Say it again."

should your body fall apart
every star and firefly
you leave behind
will come home

RED SPIDER

NGC 6543

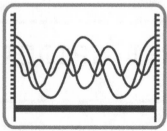

TREBLE

OORT
CLOUD

AUTO
PILOT

WARP
REFUEL

EXIT
MILKY WAY

BASS

"So this is where
stars are born."

NOT IN THIS CASE

"I thought all nebulae were
the birthplace of stars."

EXCEPT FOR PLANETARY NEBULAE,
WHICH IS WHAT NGC 6543 IS

"Do they only
create planets?"

NEGATIVE
NEITHER STARS OR PLANETS ARE
FORMED IN PLANETARY NEBULAE

"Well, if nothing
is created, then what
happens inside them?"

THIS IS WHERE STARS DIE

POWER

TRAJ

TUNER

VOLUME

NGC 6543 INTERFACE

TREBLE

OORT
CLOUD

AUTO
PILOT

WARP
REFUEL

EXIT
MILKY WAY

BASS

senses intensified
dreams magnified
visions verified
tongue tied
cat's eye

soft-spoken lullabies
counterclockwise
sunset skies
no goodbyes
butterfly

low oxygen supply
shooting fireflies
electrified
fucking horrified

PLEASE STAND BY

you and I
unified
inside
the swan eye

POWER

TRAJ

TUNER

VOLUME

CAT'S EYE

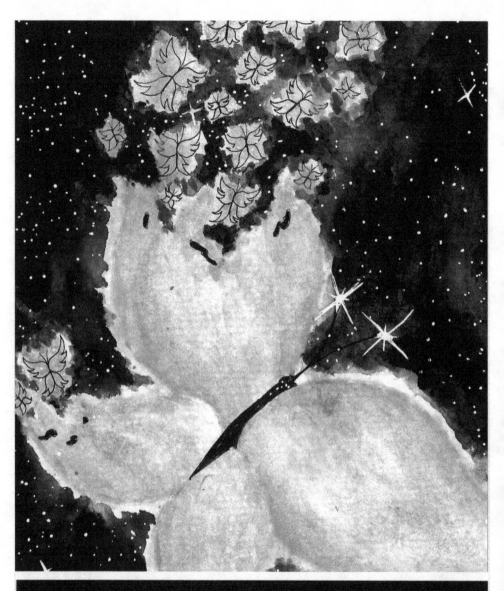

NGC 6302

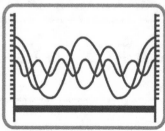

"What are we going to do?"

THERE IS NOTHING
TO BE SCARED OF
YOU HAVE MADE
IT THIS FAR

"I'm fucking terrified. How
will we get passed it without
it attacking the vessel?"

ACCORDING TO THE ARCHIVES,
BUTTERFLY WINGS ARE
EXTREMELY DELICATE

"Are you saying we should
just fly just through it?
Won't that anger it?"

I DO NOT THINK INSECTS HAD
EMOTIONS TO SPEAK OF,
EVEN IF THEY COULD SPEAK

"Lucky for them."

YOU WILL BE FINE

"What makes you so sure?"

YOU JUST HAVE
TO TRUST ME

NGC 6302 INTERFACE

TREBLE

OORT
CLOUD

AUTO
PILOT

WARP
REFUEL

EXIT
MILKY WAY

POWER

TRAJ

TUNER

VOLUME

change one thing
change everything
what will be the cost
to regain what was lost?

YOU GET WHAT YOU PAY FOR

thousands of years spent
gazing into remnants
phosphorescent snowflakes
twinkle on wisps of solar wind

they tumble and drift
down your hourglass
one glowing crystal at a time
until you appear in the dunes

your inner star,
the most beautiful in the galaxy,
almost undetectable
beneath your torus of dust

still, I felt the heat
of your caged heart
rising, escaping
from the depths of you

"Please. Don't leave me."

BASS

BUTTERFLY

TREBLE

OORT
CLOUD

AUTO
PILOT

WARP
REFUEL

EXIT
MILKY WAY

BASS

as I tried to salvage
your fading flame
a swarm of insect wings
snuffed out the wick

the smoke was everywhere
I couldn't breathe
I didn't want to see
metamorphosis complete

emerge from your chrysalis
I wouldn't change a thing
I wouldn't change anything
about you

POWER

TRAJ

TUNER

VOLUME

LEDA 3074547

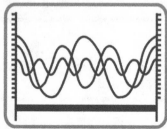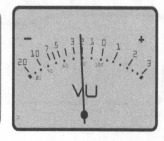

TREBLE

OORT
CLOUD

AUTO
PILOT

WARP
REFUEL

EXIT
MILKY WAY

BASS

"The vessel's heating units
s-s-seem to be malf-functioning.
It's f-f-freezing in here all
of a sudden."

WE ARE PASSING LEDA 3074547.
IT IS THE COLDEST OBJECT
IN THE GALAXY

"How c-cold exactly?"

ONE DEGREE ABOVE
ABSOLUTE ZERO

"It feels like th-th-there's
a p-p-presence here with us.
Like someone b-b-breathing
down my n-n-neck."

SEEING AS WE ARE
THE ONLY TWO ON BOARD,
THIS IS QUITE IMPOSSIBLE

"M-maybe she's here. M-maybe
she's t-t-trying to reach me."

I WILL HAVE THE HEATERS
INSPECTED. YOU SHOULD PUT ON
YOUR SUIT IN THE MEANTIME

"I can f-f-feel her
fingers on my s-s-spine."

TRY TO RELAX

POWER

TRAJ

TUNER

VOLUME

LEDA 3074547 INTERFACE

TREBLE

OORT
CLOUD

AUTO
PILOT

WARP
REFUEL

EXIT
MILKY WAY

BASS

the shivers
always
come back

from the bottom
of my spine
to the back of my neck

I freeze
you appear
I can't move
you start to fade

I thaw
you're gone
come back
I need you

the shivers
always
come back

BOOMERANG

NGC 6611

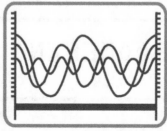

TREBLE

OORT CLOUD

AUTO PILOT

WARP REFUEL

EXIT MILKY WAY

POWER

TRAJ

TUNER

VOLUME

"They're so beautiful."

THESE ARE THE PILLARS OF
CREATION, ONE OF THE MOST
RECOGNIZEABLE CELESTIAL
STRUCTURES IN THE GALAXY

"I have this strange sense that I
should pay my respects to
these...space deities."

I THOUGHT YOU DID NOT BELIEVE
IN THAT SORT OF THING

"When you're in the prescence of
something so majestic, you can't
help but fall to your knees."

BASS

M16 INTERFACE

TREBLE

OORT
CLOUD

AUTO
PILOT

WARP
REFUEL

EXIT
MILKY WAY

BASS

POWER

TRAJ

TUNER

VOLUME

let's make music together
in the halls of our Pantheon
only us and the hydrogen columns
towering over us like
an audience of silent titans

reverberating
throughout our temple
their bass tones the tempo
to our meteoric waltz
as we drift over the cloudtops

PILLARS OF CREATION

NGC 7635

 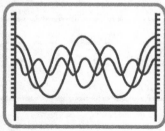 

TREBLE

OORT
CLOUD

AUTO
PILOT

WARP
REFUEL

EXIT
MILKY WAY

BASS

"You think we'll be
alright flying so close?"

YES, THERE IS NO
DANGER HERE

"But what if it pops?
The shockwave could
knock us off course."

DO YOU THINK YOU ARE TAKING
THE NAMES OF THESE NEBULAE
A BIT TOO LITERALLY?

"No, why?"

NO REASON

POWER

TRAJ

TUNER

VOLUME

NGC 7635 INTERFACE

TREBLE

OORT
CLOUD

AUTO
PILOT

WARP
REFUEL

EXIT
MILKY WAY

BASS

POWER

TRAJ

TUNER

VOLUME

I should really
wear my glasses more
even you say I look better
cuter
sexier
with them on

but there's something
about the world being
out of focus
bubbles of bokeh
in different shades
of color and light

scurrying
like neon caterpillars
as we drive above the metropolis
that lets me see everything
clearly

BUBBLES

MyCn 18

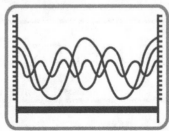

TREBLE

OORT CLOUD

AUTO PILOT

WARP REFUEL

EXIT MILKY WAY

BASS

"We're running out of time!
Can't we go any faster?"

WE MUST FOLLOW THE TRAJECTORY
FOR PROPER REFUELING OTHERWISE
WE WILL NOT MAKE IT TO CYGNUS A

"But what if we get there
and she's already gone?
I can't lose her again!"

YOU DO NOT EVEN KNOW IF
SHE IS THERE AT ALL

"She's there. I know it."

HOW CAN YOU BE SO SURE?

"Because it's all I have
left to believe in."

POWER

TRAJ

TUNER

VOLUME

MyCn 18 INTERFACE

TREBLE

OORT
CLOUD

AUTO
PILOT

WARP
REFUEL

EXIT
MILKY WAY

BASS

slipping away
through a portal
from the present
to the past

have to stay
make me immortal
in timelines bent
molds with cracks

falling ice crystals
my Olympus Mons
is forming below
Cygnus A above

glass nearly full
sleep until dawn
mountain of snow
silhouettes you, love

POWER

TRAJ

TUNER

VOLUME

HOURGLASS

NGC 3372

 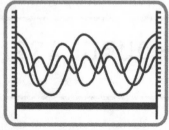 

TREBLE

OORT
CLOUD

AUTO
PILOT

WARP
REFUEL

EXIT
MILKY WAY

BASS

"This is the end.
We can't go on."

I DO NOT UNDERSTAND

"The gate is locked. We need
a key to get through."

THERE ARE NO GATES ON BOARD
THE VESSEL AND NONE OF THE
HATCHES OR AIRLOCKS REQUIRE
KEYS, AT LEAST NOT THE ONES
YOU ARE THINKING OF

"I'm not talking about the
ship. That gate outside,
straight ahead."

YOU MEAN THE NEBULA?

"I know what I'm looking at!
How will we get through
without a key?"

...WHAT ABOUT THE VESSEL?

"What about it?"

WHAT IF THE
VESSEL IS THE KEY?

"You really think?"

ONLY ONE WAY TO BE SURE

POWER

TRAJ

TUNER

VOLUME

NGC 3372 INTERFACE

TREBLE

OORT
CLOUD

AUTO
PILOT

WARP
REFUEL

EXIT
MILKY WAY

BASS

POWER

TRAJ

TUNER

VOLUME

unlock the music box
the hologram of the dancer
a pixelated princess
spins like a neutron star
faster and faster

her gown, a record
of light and dust
on an unseen turntable
oh, how that dancer glows
oh, how that music grows

louder and louder
it's so beautiful
like the soundtrack
of a film about us
with you and I as the stars

          "You were always
           my shining star."

brighter and brighter
the dancer glows

          "I won't look away
           and I won't blink."

she's so luminous
as the light
pulsates from her chest
and swallows her

THE KEYHOLE

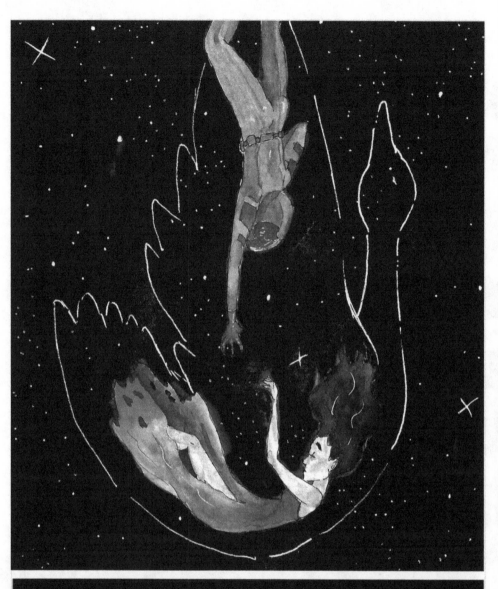

SN 1671

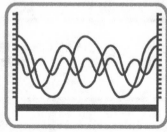

TREBLE

POWER

OORT
CLOUD

TRAJ

AUTO
PILOT

"This is absolutely
breathtaking."

I AM SURE IT WAS EVEN MORE SO
BEFORE IT EXPLODED

WARP
REFUEL

"Before?"

TUNER

THIS IS A SUPERNOVA REMNANT, THE
REMAINS OF AN EXPLODED STAR
FROM SEVERAL THOUSAND YEARS AGO

EXIT
MILKY WAY

"So...it's the corpse
of a corpse?"

VOLUME

I GUESS YOU COULD SAY THAT

BASS

SN 1671 INTERFACE

TREBLE

POWER

swan princess
my name for you
though, these days
your monarchy
reigns no more

the first and last
of its species
indexed and cataloged
in your ornithology

in a cage
of glass bones
and paper skin

with fractured wing
and dimming white dwarf

I dive

OORT
CLOUD

AUTO
PILOT

WARP
REFUEL

EXIT
MILKY WAY

TRAJ

TUNER

VOLUME

BASS

CASSIOPEIA A

BOÖTES VOID

 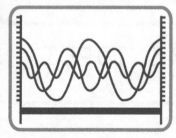 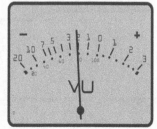

TREBLE

OORT
CLOUD

AUTO
PILOT

WARP
REFUEL

EXIT
MILKY WAY

BASS

"We're not going in there
...are we?"

NEGATIVE, THIS IS MERELY A FLYBY.
NOTHING IN THE SUPERVOID IS
REQUIRED TO PROCEED
WITH THE MISSION

If I had not been debriefed on
Cygnus A and shown images prior
to departure, I would have
thought this was the black hole."

FROM A DIFFERENT PERSPECTIVE,
THIS MAY, IN FACT, BE WORSE
THAN CYGNUS A

"Worse how?"

AS YOU KNOW, CHANCES OF SURVIVING
ENTRANCE TO A BLACK HOLE
ARE INFINITELY SLIM

"Thank you for that
pleasant reminder."

IN A SUPERVOID, HOWEVER, YOU
WOULD CERTAINLY MAKE IT INSIDE,
BUT DUE TO ITS VAST EMPTINESS,
YOUR PRESENCE WOULD BE UNKNOWN TO
ANYONE OUTSIDE ITS BORDERS FOR
CENTURIES

"That's fucking terrifying."

AGAIN, IT IS ALL
A MATTER OF PERSPECTIVE

POWER

TRAJ

TUNER

VOLUME

BOÖTES VOID INTERFACE

TREBLE

OORT
CLOUD

AUTO
PILOT

WARP
REFUEL

EXIT
MILKY WAY

BASS

POWER

TRAJ

TUNER

VOLUME

there is a sort of nothing
that has come from nowhere
where the answers
are given by nobody
and received by
no one

but I'll tell you something
out there somewhere
there will always be
somebody waiting
and I believe you are that
someone

BOÖTES VOID

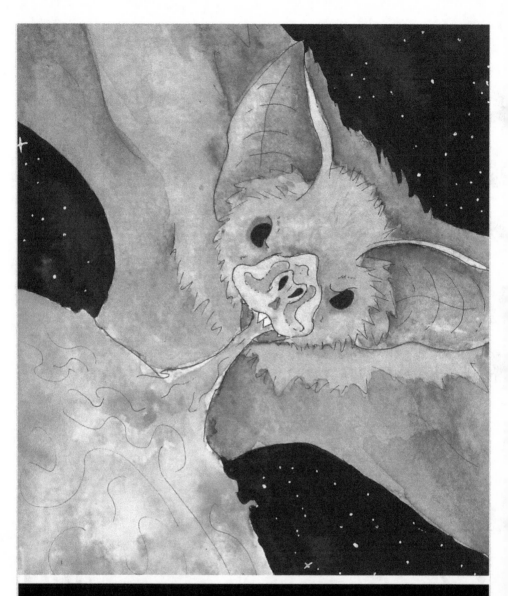

SS LEPORIS

 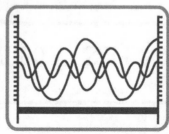 

TREBLE

OORT CLOUD

AUTO PILOT

WARP REFUEL

EXIT MILKY WAY

BASS

"This can't be happening.
This can't be happening.
This can't be happening."

REMEMBER TO TAKE DEEP SLOW
BREATHS.
WHATEVER YOU SEE, IT IS NOT REAL
NONE OF IT IS REAL

"I can't do this! I can't! It's
too much! These horrors! These
nightmares! They're never going
to end. None of it is ever going
to fucking end!"

THINK ABOUT WHAT YOU ARE SAYING
REMEMBER WHY YOU ARE HERE

"I take take this anymore! I
can't! I just fucking can't!"

LISTEN TO ME
YOU HAVE TO GET THROUGH THIS
THINK ABOUT LUCY
SHE IS STILL OUT THERE
WAITING FOR YOU

"...Lucy...I'm sorry.
I miss you so fucking much."

THEN DO NOT KEEP HER WAITING
GO AND GET HER

POWER

TRAJ

TUNER

VOLUME

SS LEPORIS INTERFACE

POWER

TRAJ

TREBLE

OORT
CLOUD

AUTO
PILOT

take my life
straight from my throat
take your time
make it slow

TUNER

WARP
REFUEL

lyrics from my eulogy
drawn from the wounds
crimson wax bleeds
over love letters in blue

EXIT
MILKY WAY

creature of the black
raised by the stars
lay me in the tesseract
and let my shadows crawl

VOLUME

BASS

CREATURE

TREBLE

OORT
CLOUD

AUTO
PILOT

WARP
REFUEL

EXIT
MILKY WAY

POWER

TRAJ

TUNER

"How long was I asleep?"

YOU HAVE NOT SLEPT IN 19 HOURS.

VOLUME

BASS

INTERFACE

TREBLE

OORT CLOUD

AUTO PILOT

WARP REFUEL

EXIT MILKY WAY

POWER

TRAJ

TUNER

VOLUME

the way you dance
a carousel spinning
at the hands of a madman
I thought I saw you
wink at me from afar
through my clouded visor

          IMAGE ENHANCEMENT FAILURE

my dancing princess
twirling with the filth
of the universe
embrace me in your arms of dust
my head spinning
like the carousel

just when I think
we're going to collide
you
      pass
          right
              through
                    me

become my symbiote
a temporary possession

        "You're moving too fast!
          I can't hold on!"

slipping further
and further
and further away
into the eternal night

BASS

GHOST GALAXIES

POWER

TREBLE

TRAJ

OORT
CLOUD

AUTO
PILOT

TUNER

WARP
REFUEL

EXIT
MILKY WAY

VOLUME

BASS

your eyes burn
casting away the darkness
with your fiery gaze
the shadows that drowned you
in their waves
of sleepwalking terror
retreat to the safety
of the hollow
gathering their strength
for the next onslaught
against your pure white light

your eyes still rage
like the Supernova of 1006
the wavelengths of your irises
collide with the forces
of the night
the words to our secret songs
echo like violent whispers
between the Pillars of Creation
and the melodies' luminescence
leaves the dust
and the Dark
quivering

PHOTOEVAPORATION

TREBLE

OORT
CLOUD

AUTO
PILOT

WARP
REFUEL

EXIT
MILKY WAY

BASS

where did we leave off
in the fairy tale nightmare?
did we eat the poisoned apple
or prick our finger
on the accursed spindle?

drifting into unconsciousness
eyes weigh down
bricks from the Pillars
falling like burning meteors
and I cannot resist
the urge to sleep

and behind my weary eyes
you emerge from the depths
of my mind's casket
my darling of the divine
this does not feel like a dream
but wish for you to follow me

when I wake

POWER

TRAJ

TUNER

VOLUME

SLEEPING WITH BEAUTY

TREBLE

OORT
CLOUD

AUTO
PILOT

WARP
REFUEL

EXIT
MILKY WAY

BASS

the great unknown
that's where you are
you and I
two opposites
in polar attraction
tugging on my heartstrings
like an exhausted trout
struggling to fight
dark energy's mighty current

your pull is weak
often
nearly undetectable
but I still hold on
I'll always hold on
as you had always done
for me

POWER

TRAJ

TUNER

VOLUME

THE GREAT ATTRACTOR

TREBLE

OORT
CLOUD

AUTO
PILOT

WARP
REFUEL

EXIT
MILKY WAY

BASS

POWER

TRAJ

TUNER

VOLUME

I'm sure at one point,
I belonged to the star system
of my ancestors
following ancient orbital paths
in planetary gardens,
warmed by our golden sol
and that pale dreamcatcher,
hanging from a sheet
of pinhole-velvet

I know at one point,
I was infected
by an undeniable urge
the world I knew,
so empty and plain
you only exist in my dreams
subconscious alleviates
visions of you transcend
sitcom reruns in my head

I've reached
the point of epiphany
this star system cannot hold me
quantum entanglement
in space-time fabric
update "WANDERLUST"
to "WANDERLOST"
a nomadic quest
for some cause or reason
everything I've come to know
of a place I used to call home

ROGUE PLANET

TREBLE

OORT
CLOUD

AUTO
PILOT

WARP
REFUEL

EXIT
MILKY WAY

POWER

TRAJ

TUNER

there is a new home
I know there is
somewhere between the lines
of star maps and time
and the verses
of our hearts' pulses
and that home is you

VOLUME

BASS

CYGNUS A TRAJECTORY
PHASE FIVE: CYGNUS A

TREBLE

CYGNUS
A

PHOTON
SPHERE

EVENT
HORIZON

BASS

POWER

TRAJ

TUNER

VOLUME

"The gravity
of the situation
has finally struck me."

NOW IS NOT THE
TIME FOR JOKES

"I don't know if
I'm ready for this."

NO ONE EVER IS

CYGNUS A INTERFACE

TREBLE

CYGNUS A

PHOTON SPHERE

EVENT HORIZON

BASS

the sky is full of ghosts, love
I navigate endlessly
like a lost nomad
through this mausoleum

with my vessel as my mortuary
I'll watch
and I'll wait
as my daydreams become
weightless

Jupiter is for lovers like us
wraiths of ice and stone
all the stars
we used to connect us
were gone
long before either of us
arrived to this place

POWER

TRAJ

TUNER

VOLUME

CYGNUS A

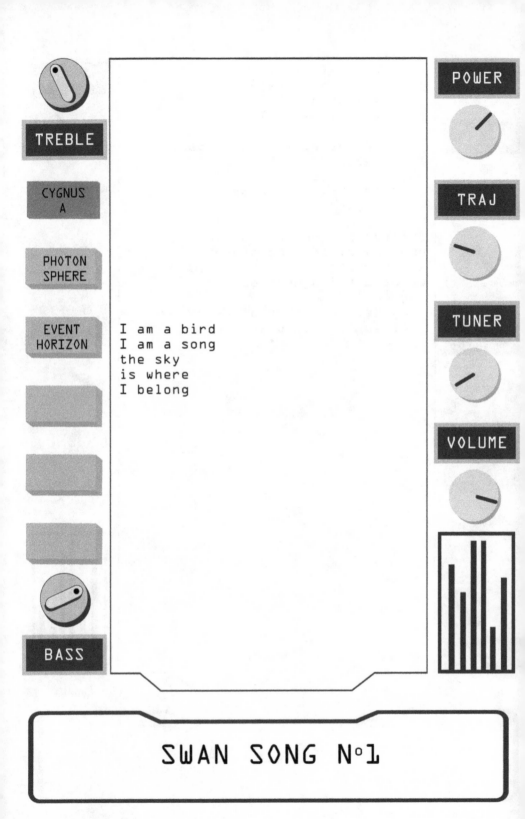

TREBLE

CYGNUS
A

PHOTON
SPHERE

EVENT
HORIZON

POWER

TRAJ

TUNER

VOLUME

I.
born of fire and ice
our particles became one
at opposite ends of the wreckage
the dark energy stretched
but gravity took us by the hand
and made us something more
and it was then we danced
it was then we glowed

II.
we share the same sky
eclipse the same moon
make poets cry
and lovers swoon
synchronized ballet
in this ocean, we swim
two spherical flames
in gravitational spins

BASS

BINARY STAR SYSTEM I

TREBLE

CYGNUS
A

PHOTON
SPHERE

EVENT
HORIZON

POWER

TRAJ

TUNER

VOLUME

beauty and her beast
this decadent dance
one last chance
before the feast

assimilation complete
x-rays emitted
ultraviolet, infrared
feathers frayed, no retreat

BASS

BINARY STAR SYSTEM II

TREBLE

CYGNUS A

PHOTON SPHERE

EVENT HORIZON

BASS

words scratched by my nails
and the tip of the pen
stained in the ink of squids
flourishing like vapor trails
across a sky of white

all the photo albums
in the back of my mind
are brought to light
in front of me
watching the projector
change slides
one flashback after another

and the Black Swan
slowly comes into view
you're just as beautiful
as I remember

POWER

TRAJ

TUNER

VOLUME

BLACK HOLE BOHEMIAN

TREBLE

CYGNUS
A

PHOTON
SPHERE

EVENT
HORIZON

BASS

POWER

TRAJ

TUNER

VOLUME

water evaporates
slowly erased
identity replaced
relic in a suitcase

incomplete
time fleets
death cheats
sweat-stained sheets

running out of time

　　　　YOU WILL BE FINE

your boy of blue skies

　　"I am not afraid to die."

awaiting the crow
whispering willows
moons of Pluto
more tomorrows

tattoos at 22
the Challenger crew
the sky is always blue
I will always love you

HAWKING RADIATION

TREBLE

CYGNUS
A

PHOTON
SPHERE

EVENT
HORIZON

BASS

record spinning
billions of rpms
needle drops
sparkling notes
bouncing pinballs

rings of ice and rock
overture of the oblivion
striking barren exoplanets
far beyond the reach
of my satellites and fingertips

melody echoes in our lungs
all we can breathe
a love of lyric and song
that neither of us
would ever resist

POWER

TRAJ

TUNER

VOLUME

ACCRETION DISK

TREBLE

CYGNUS A

PHOTON SPHERE

EVENT HORIZON

BASS

migrations and mirages
from my home
to the edge
and back again
into your dreams

taking in what memories I can
from the remains
of our constellations
and swallow them like a heron

abandon our nest
constructed atop the clouds
Icarus descending
the only thing to do
before this enigma of endeavors
is to keep on loving you

POWER

TRAJ

TUNER

VOLUME

SWAN SONG Nº2

TREBLE

CYGNUS
A

PHOTON
SPHERE

EVENT
HORIZON

BASS

a spoonful of this plague
will grab hold of us
and never stop pulling
tangled in the terrible tentacles
of a celestial cephalopod

there will be no escape, love
nothing I do
can prevent this leviathan
from taking me down with you

now I'm more blue
than I've ever been
I told you I'd never let go
I never thought
it would be like this

POWER

TRAJ

TUNER

VOLUME

NEUTRON STAR

POWER

TREBLE

TRAJ

CYGNUS
A

PHOTON
SPHERE

TUNER

EVENT
HORIZON

VOLUME

BASS

```
watching helplessly
as the burden and sickness
that defied all panacea
weighed heavily on you

the further you collapsed
the more I was drawn to you
gravitational forces so strong
I couldn't leave your bedside

I always knew I would find you
you were my beacon
on a jagged shore
by a sea of nightmares and ink

I held your hand
your pulse diminishing
your skin cooling
a little each day

        "I will find you."

          "I know."
```

PULSAR

TREBLE

CYGNUS
A

PHOTON
SPHERE

EVENT
HORIZON

BASS

POWER

TRAJ

TUNER

VOLUME

```
you pulled me in
and I can't leave you
you've got me running
running circles around you
and I can't leave you
you set my body
        heart
            and soul
                ablaze
and with starless eyes
you stared

you pulled me in
and I can't leave you
I'm a rag doll
in a space suit
and I can't leave you
seeing the same shadows
        again
            and again
                and again
unaware
they were being cast by me

you pulled me in
and I can't leave you
we are suspended
in our meteoric waltz
and I can't leave you
I ignite and I burn
        brighter
            and hotter
                and faster
and you stare, black
and deep
with your starless eyes
and I can't leave you
```

MAGNETAR

TREBLE

POWER

CYGNUS
A

TRAJ

PHOTON
SPHERE

TUNER

EVENT
HORIZON

VOLUME

BASS

silence is the enemy
invading my ears
to eradicate all the sounds
that remind me of you

your laugh
sweet and contagious
your sigh
as you slowly collapse onto me

and all the words
you've ever spoken
all the songs
you've ever sung

our song still endures
the symphony of the universe
blazes through the void
left in my heart

a beam of radio waves
across lightyears and yesteryears
I hear it on the vessel radio
and can't help but sing along

QUASAR

TREBLE

CYGNUS
A

PHOTON
SPHERE

EVENT
HORIZON

POWER

TRAJ

TUNER

VOLUME

billions of lightyears away
you called to me
with your starlight stare

pulses of your heartbeat
radiate with love and memory
back to a time before time

we dwelled in silent darkness
until that first spark ignited
and blazed on for eternity

BASS

BLAZAR

POWER

TREBLE

CYGNUS
A

TRAJ

PHOTON
SPHERE

EVENT
HORIZON

TUNER

VOLUME

BASS

```
a future now past
smash the mold
from the poured cast
I told myself

          "There will be
        no one like you,
      now or ever to come."

peripheral vision
deceived me
gamma incision
relieved me

a heart vitrified
left to freeze
now revived
brighter than the Pleiades
```

GAMMA RAY BURST

even in death, you shone
brighter than Sirius A
everything you kept inside
all the Dark
all the light

detonated
resonated

your dazzling carcass
spilled watercolor entrails
across the emptiness of myself
and for a brief moment
I was blinded by you

you were so beautiful
and still, even in death,
I gaze upon the shimmering lights
of your resurrected corpse
and smile

HYPERNOVA

TREBLE

CYGNUS A

PHOTON SPHERE

EVENT HORIZON

BASS

it's an odd feeling
the day you choose
your own cryotube

the make and model
the perfect fit
future interstellar trip

the gold plate etched
with name and years
somehow easy
to hold back tears

it'll be an odd feeling
the day I sleep
in a cryotube
made just for me

POWER

TRAJ

TUNER

VOLUME

CRYOTUBE C

TREBLE

CYGNUS A

PHOTON SPHERE

EVENT HORIZON

BASS

POWER

TRAJ

TUNER

VOLUME

we are two swans
eternally bound
pure white coats
and feather crowns

songs cooed
on a lake of stars
gamma ray bursts
supernova sparks

ripples echo
echo like radio waves
playing our song
to the rhythm of solar rays

the Big Bang
the rings of Saturn
love and chaos
have a similar pattern

hand in hand
wing to wing
through the Pillars
our hearts will ring

fly like Hermes
love like Virgo
and we'll never let go
I'll never let go

run my fingers
in your aurora hair
I love how
your pixel eyes stare

long and deep
hypnotized
you make me want to be
alive

SWAN SONG Nº3

TREBLE

CYGNUS
A

PHOTON
SPHERE

EVENT
HORIZON

BASS

POWER

TRAJ

TUNER

VOLUME

```
my heartbeat
is slow
and
it's getting
dark

our love's
arpeggio
is played
on vibrations
of stars

chemistry
reacts
love flows like
O and H₂

gravitons
attract
like me to
you
```

my heartbeat
is slow
and
it's getting
dark

our love's
arpeggio
is played
on vibrations
of stars

chemistry
reacts
love flows like
O and H_2

gravitons
attract
like me to
you

GRAVITONS

TREBLE

CYGNUS
A

PHOTON
SPHERE

EVENT
HORIZON

BASS

what's yours
is mine
is hours

holding on
hands together
for all time

our voices, the chimes
orchestrating every new hour
and every new day

I wind up your music box
ticking like a metronome
a pause, and then it plays

you are eternity
I am infinity
we are forever

POWER

TRAJ

TUNER

VOLUME

CHRONONS

TREBLE

CYGNUS
A

PHOTON
SPHERE

EVENT
HORIZON

POWER

TRAJ

TUNER

VOLUME

eroding marble goddess
lips red to supergiant blue
white dwarf skin
to thundercloud gray
materialize at the rendezvous

almost my corpse bride
in tattered rags and veil
a bouquet of wilted roses
and comet tails

pulsar to magnetar
colliding with your kiss
ripples in your Regulus orbs
resurrected from the abyss

Bellatrix eyes
do not erase
before one last dream
one last embrace

BASS

RENDEZVOUS

TREBLE

CYGNUS
A

PHOTON
SPHERE

EVENT
HORIZON

BASS

you are time
passing infinitely
into the future
leaving me in the present
unable to follow

I am space
stretching forever
across the abysmal wilderness
until the day we meet again

because you and I
are not separate entities
but one embodiment
of the same soul

POWER

TRAJ

TUNER

VOLUME

RELATIVITY

TREBLE

CYGNUS
A

PHOTON
SPHERE

EVENT
HORIZON

BASS

running out of time
to preserve everything of you
I've collected
since our beginning

the closer I'm drawn to you
the more the Dark takes away
remodeling our museum
into a morgue

once I fall into you
I'll finally be free
yet it terrifies me
as all the light is digested
my heart cold and lifeless

motionless but patient
I, a dormant comet
on the edge of night
soon to be awoken
by your solar flares once more

POWER

TRAJ

TUNER

VOLUME

SCHWARZCHILD RADIUS

TREBLE

CYGNUS
A

PHOTON
SPHERE

EVENT
HORIZON

POWER

TRAJ

TUNER

VOLUME

set the vessel to hover
prepare the shuttle
I glimpse out my window
and suddenly, anesthetized
by her swan eye

"I could stare
into you
forever."

YOU DID NOT COME HERE
FOR THE VIEW

I told you I'd be back, love
open your arms and let me fall
headfirst and smiling
into your black beauty

"I've waited so long
for this moment."

BASS

EVENT HORIZON

when in space
there can be beautiful nebulae
and hungry black holes

        DEPENDING WHICH DIRECTION
    YOU ARE LOOKING OUT THE VESSEL

I tend to go between windows
but the black holes
fascinate me the most

unrelenting, eternal
devouring the light
and everything else

I'm hypnotized
as it stares, unforgiving
into the depths of me

and I wonder
which one of us
is being swallowed

EVERYTHING ELSE

TREBLE

CYGNUS A

PHOTON SPHERE

EVENT HORIZON

BASS

they'll be a temporary period
my sweet pixel queen
when I'll wander aimlessly
through haunted dreams of ghosts
and underexposed photographs

a hermit, trekking forests
of junipers and magnolias
wading effervescent creeks
skipping stones
over lakes of glass

but for all we know
there could be a road overgrown
with anemone and begonias
coated in comet snow
with familiar footprints
to follow home

POWER

TRAJ

TUNER

VOLUME

EINSTEIN-ROSEN BRIDGE

TREBLE

CYGNUS
A

PHOTON
SPHERE

EVENT
HORIZON

POWER

TRAJ

TUNER

VOLUME

I let the star dust bury me
plummeting into the void
memories become constellations
maps to places
further than I'll ever go

my boots in the clutches
of mighty claws
the beast hides
deep inside the Dark
and waits

s   t   i   t   c   h   e   s

l   i   m   b   s

a   t   o   m   s

u   n   d   o   n   e

I can only be pulled
so far
before being
ripped a   p   a   r   t

BASS

SPAGHETTIFICATION

TREBLE

CYGNUS
A

PHOTON
SPHERE

EVENT
HORIZON

BASS

it's all come to this
my swan princess
I close my eyes
and see more than I ever did
since my first sunrise

everything we are
everything we were
everything we will ever be

you and I
infinitely free
you and I
at our singularity

POWER

TRAJ

TUNER

VOLUME

SINGULARITY

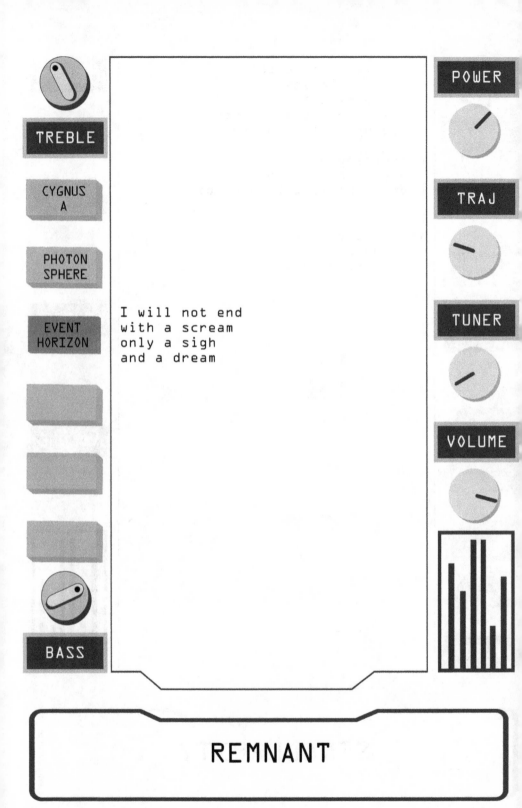

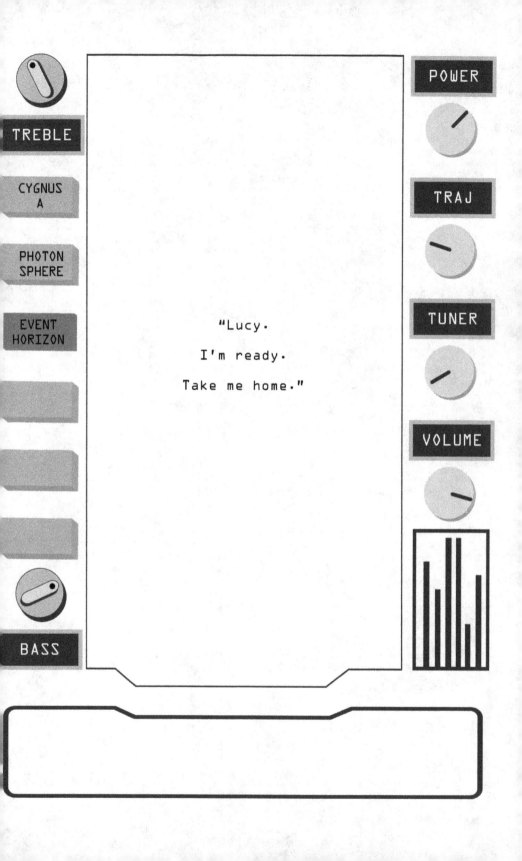

ARE YOU ALRIGHT?

"Who's there?"

"How did this happen?"

ALL THE FLIGHT RECORDERS
MALFUNCTIONED DURING ENTRY.
THERE'S NO WAY TO KNOW

"So we have no idea where we are?"

UNFORTUNATELY

"When did we get out?"

OF THE BLACK HOLE?

"No, the ship."

WE HAVEN'T LEFT THE SHIP

IT APPEARS THE SHIP
HAS PICKED UP SOME KIND
OF LOW FREQUENCY SOUND

"From where?"

STRANGE

"What is it?"

THAT LOW FREQUENCY SOUND

"What about it?"

IT'S A VOICE

I want to go back
but I feel it's already too late
sometimes they say
it's better to wait

                    how can I reach tomorrow
                            if it never comes?
                    how can I go back to yesterday
                        when today is already done?

the future, an endless void
all satellites and probes have been deployed
failed transmissions
what's the price of admission
for one last chance

                        for one last dance?

push reset

let's try this one more time
my little clementine
I can't do this on my own
I made sure to remember my lines

JESSICA KRETZENGER PHOTOGRAPHY

VINCENT HOLLOW is an astropoet and interstellar storyteller living aboard the space vessel. Aquarius. Shooting from star system to star system. Vincent spends his time gazing out into the universal abyss and the depths of himself where he hopes to find his place in the cosmos through the words he weaves in the fabric of spacetime.

CPSIA information can be obtained
at www.ICGtesting.com
Printed in the USA
BVHW071241161120
593415BV00003B/38